Comparing Sporting Nations

For Kaitlyn, Abbey and Avery

–Mathew Dowling

For Mona, Maya and Arlo

–Spencer Harris

Mathew Dowling and Spencer Harris

COMPARING
SPORTING
NATIONS

THEORY AND METHOD

Meyer & Meyer Sport

British Library Cataloguing in Publication Data
A catalogue record for this book is available from the British Library

Comparing Sporting Nations
Maidenhead: Meyer & Meyer Sport (UK) Ltd., 2021
ISBN: 978-1-78255-216-1

Aachen, Auckland, Beirut, Cairo, Cape Town, Dubai, Hägendorf, Hong Kong, Indianapolis, Maidenhead, Manila, New Delhi, Singapore, Sydney, Tehran, Vienna

Member of the World Sport Publishers' Association (WSPA), www.w-s-p-a.org

Printed by: CPI – Clausen & Bosse, Leck
Printed in Germany

ISBN: 978-1-78255-216-1

Email: info@m-m-sports.com
www.thesportspublisher.com

CONTENTS

LIST OF FIGURES

LIST OF TABLES

LIST OF CASE STUDIES

ACKNOWLEDGEMENTS

It is not possible to produce such a volume of work without accruing a large number of debts and relying upon the generous goodwill of others. In particular, we would like to acknowledge all those who were kind enough to entertain our curiousity and expand our thinking further, either over email or coffee, and to those colleagues – especially Ian Henry, Jonathan Grix, David Legg, Marvin Washington, Aaron Beacom and Phil Brown – who have been integral and supportive in helping us shape our thoughts.

We would also like to thank Liz Evans (Meyer & Meyer Sport) and Amanda Arbuthnot for their support throughout the process and proofreading the manuscript, and the many colleagues including Verity Allen, Danny Cullinane, James Johnstone, Becca Leopkey, Jonathan Robertson, Alex Thurston, Chris Mackintosh, Katrina McDonald, and Verity Postlethwaite who were kind enough to review our chapters. Finally, a personal thanks and gratitude to our partners and children whom without this work would not be possible.

INTRODUCTION

THE LOGIC OF COMPARATIVE INQUIRY IN SPORT

Chapter objectives

- To outline the importance and utility of the comparative method;
- To provide an overview of the logic of comparative inquiry within sport;
- To begin to explore the challenges and limitations of comparing sporting nations.

It is the essence of human nature to compare, and making comparisons is an essential part of understanding and interpreting society. As social entities, we make comparisons every day and throughout each stage of life. Children develop through comparison by copying and imitating others. Teenagers compare themselves to their peers and social media influencers to see whether they are keeping up with the latest trends. Adults compare the price and quality of products when shopping online, spend countless hours using comparison websites to buy home or car insurance, and generally compare their own lives and benchmark their social standing to their neighbours – hence the idiom 'keeping up with the Joneses'. Restaurants are reviewed and ranked according to food critics through web-based companies. Schools are inspected and compared by government agencies or professional bodies. Universities are ranked and compared using league tables and so on. In short, comparisons are everywhere. This book focuses on a particular type of comparison at the organisational and trans-national level – comparing sporting nations.

Despite its common everyday usage, however, what exactly are comparisons? What does it mean to compare? As a logical starting point, most dictionary definitions describe 'to compare' as a transitive verb, i.e., an action with an associated object. Collins English Dictionary, for example, states: "When you compare things, you consider them and discover the difference and similarities between them". Similarly, for Merriam-Webster, to compare is to

1. represent as similar;
2. examine the character or qualities of, especially to discover resemblances or differences;
3. view in relation to.

What can be drawn from these definitions is that to compare is to observe and examine one object or thing in relation to another. Broadly speaking, comparative research can be understood as an attempt to compare two or more things based upon empirical observation to make inferences or generalisations about social phenomena. Some sociologists and political scientists equate the scientific method with the comparative method. Such perspectives do not differentiate between the comparative method and other forms of sociological inquiry. Thus, all sociological inquiry attempts to make comparisons between phenomena, whether the unit of analysis is comparing individuals, organisations, or nations. Some scholars have argued that all social sciences, whether comparing different social groups, phenomena or behaviour, are based upon comparisons. As Øyen (1990) notes, "no social phenomenon can be isolated and studied without comparing it to other social phenomena. Sociologists engage actively in the process of comparative work whenever concepts are chosen, operationalized or fitted into theoretical structures" (Øyen, 1990, p. 4). It can be argued, therefore, that any empirical observation involves some level of comparison. It is perhaps for this reason that the famous sociologist Émile Durkheim (1938) argued that "comparative sociology is not a particular branch of sociology: it is sociology" (p. 139). Durkheim's remarks suggest that the theoretical and methodological challenges faced by comparative researchers are fundamental to understanding the very nature of sociology itself (Jowell, 1998; Øyen, 1990).

In contrast, some view comparative analysis as a distinct form of inquiry which is unique to social sciences and can be contrasted with the experimental, statistical and case-study methods (Lijphart, 1971). According to Lijphart (1971), the comparative method shares many features with the statistical and experimental method, except the former examines phenomena whereby experimental controls are not possible because it has too few cases to be statistically significant. We will return to these issues later (see philosophical assumptions in chapter 2 and the discussion of the 'too many variables and not enough cases' problem in chapter 4). It is in this latter tradition, where the comparative method is defined as one of many scientific methods that can be employed to establish general empirical propositions and to generate knowledge, in which this book proceeds. Thus, the argument reinforced throughout this book is that the comparative method is best understood as a method of discovering empirical relationships amongst variables (in its broadest sense) and not as a specific method of measurement (Lijphart, 1971). The term itself – comparative method – is somewhat misleading in that it is not strictly a method or data collection technique *per se,* but rather, it is more accurately a broad-brush general research strategy (Lijphart, 1971). It is for this reason that some researchers prefer the terms comparative *approach* or comparative *analysis* rather than method.

Despite commonplace understandings of what it means to compare, and the established tradition of comparative methodology, it is important to recognise the ongoing difficulties and limitations of making meaningful comparisons. Conducting comparative research brings about a whole host of methodological and practical challenges and limitations that are often overlooked or even ignored by those who attempt to make comparisons within sociology and political science in general (Dogan & Pelassy, 1990; Landman & Carvalho, 2017; Lijphart, 1971; Øyen, 1990; Sartori, 1970; Schuster, 2007) and within the context of sport specifically (Dowling et al., 2018; Henry et al., 2005; Houlihan, 1997). This is why some comparative researchers have referred to comparative analysis as an 'imperfect' art and science (Øyen, 1990). Kohn (1987), for example, argues that comparative research is "costly in time and money, is difficult to do, and it often seems to raise more interpretive problems than it solves" (p. 713). Some scholars have gone so far as to describe comparative research as "plain[ly] problematic" or "deeply suspect" (Jowell, 1998, p. 176). Whilst the latter viewpoint is not shared by us, it is important to recognise the extent of the challenges faced when attempting to make meaningful (i.e., empirically grounded) comparisons. As Øyen (1990) argues:

> There is no reason to believe there exists an easy and straightforward entry into comparative social research. All the eternal and unsolved problems inherent in sociological research are unfolded when engaging in cross-national studies. None of the methodological and theoretical difficulties we have learned to live with can be ignored when we examine critically such questions as to what is comparative research, how we go about doing comparative work, and how we interpret similarities and differences in countries compared (p. 1).

The task of a comparative researcher attempting to make meaningful comparisons is therefore thwart with a series of practical and methodological challenges, pitfalls, compromises and trade-offs when making decisions about who, what, when and how to make comparisons. There is no easy or straightforward approach to comparing sporting nations. It is these challenges, limitations, and pitfalls on which this book focuses, and as will become apparent in the pages that follow, making any meaningful comparisons within sport inevitably involves a series of methodological trade-offs and/or practical compromises.

When designing comparative studies, sport researchers inevitably find themselves asking similar methodological or practical questions: how do you know that the instruments or concepts used in one country mean the same thing in others (construct equivalence)? Should the researcher consider societal, macro-level issues or focus only on system-based, meso-level factors (level of analysis)? When selecting countries, do you select based on a random sample or purposeful sample? And on what basis do you decide which countries to include and which ones to exclude in your study? How many countries should you include in your sample? Do you include as many countries as possible or only a few? How many countries should be included in the sample, given the number of independent variables employed? In carrying out a comparison, do you seek to understand the causal relationship between variables or a more detailed understanding of the socio-historical context of a case? If you take a variable-oriented approach, how many independent variables do you have in relation to the number of cases? If you take a case-based approach, do you seek to identify what is similar between these cases, what is different or both? These questions reflect the extent and breadth of the challenge that lie ahead for those wishing to make comparisons. This textbook seeks to unpack these questions in order to help make sense of this theoretical and methodological quandary and to explore further – and make more visible – the theory and method that underpin the process of making meaningful comparisons within the context of sport. A greater sense of visibility and awareness of methodological procedures is precisely what we mean by creating more 'conscious thinkers' (Sartori, 1970) of those who seek to make comparisons within the context of sport.

This is not to suggest that those who have carried out comparative analysis within sport to date are in any way 'unconscious' or are not aware of their study limitations. Many of the methodological and practical issues highlighted within this book are well-known and understood by comparative methodology scholars (Baistow, 2000; Dogan & Kazancigil, 1994; Dogan & Pelassy, 1990; Ebbinghaus, 2005; Hantrais, 2009; Jowell, 1998; Kohn, 1987; Landman & Carvalho, 2017; Lijphart, 1971; Øyen, 2004, 1990; Ragin, 2006, 2014; Sartori, 1970, 1994; Schuster, 2007). Despite this, however, many of these issues have not received the same consideration and attention within the context of sport. Consequently, there remains a dearth of literature focusing specifically on the philosophical, methodological and practical challenges of comparing sporting nations. This book builds upon, and is in many respects the culmination, of previous work with a number of colleagues which has begun to address this modest but important deficiency (Dowling, Brown, Legg, & Beacom, 2018; Dowling, Brown, Legg, & Grix, 2018; Dowling, Legg, & Brown, 2017; Harris & Dowling, *forthcoming*; Henry, Dowling, Ko, & Brown, 2020).

Furthermore, despite the difficult or seemingly impossible task that lies ahead for those who wish to undertake comparative analysis within sport, there remains no introductory textbook that explicitly focuses on and explores the theory and method of comparative analysis within the context of sport. This book seeks to address this gap in the literature by focusing on and further elucidating the theory and method of comparing sporting contexts through specific examples and case studies drawn from the comparative elite sport policy/management domain. The focus and emphasis on comparative elite sport policy/management is primarily due to the authors' background and interest in this particular sub-domain, but it also serves as a useful research context in which to examine and illustrate many of the issues identified herein.

In addition, it is also recognised that any attempt to discuss the generalities of the theory and method of comparative analysis has the potential risk of becoming too general and too abstract to be useful. It is for this reason that six illustrative case studies have been included throughout the book to demonstrate in more detail how some of these issues have (or have not) been addressed, mitigated or overcome within a particular sub-research area – the elite sport policy/management domain. Not only do they provide useful insight into the comparative elite sport policy/management domain in general, but they offer specific example reference points for the broader discussion of the theoretical and methodological issues of making comparisons. Consequently, although the book predominantly focuses upon and utilises examples drawn from the elite sport policy/management context, it is argued that the theoretical and methodological issues discussed have a much broader applicability for researchers across a wide range of sport and sport-related domains.

In recognising the current lack of explicit discussion surrounding the theory and method of comparative analysis within sport, this book also seeks to rebalance comparative sport scholars' emphasis towards explicitly acknowledging and discussing further the theory and method of comparative research which has largely been absent from the literature to date. Most sport scholars have, perhaps understandably, chosen to focus more explicitly on outlining and explaining their findings rather than discussing the theory and methods that underpin their analysis. In her seminal works, Øyen (1990) outlines a typology of the different types of social scientists involved in comparative research: *purists*, *ignorants*, *totalists*, and *comparativists*. The *purists* are those who believe that comparative analysis is no different from any other kind of sociological research. The second of Øyen's distinctions are *ignorants* – those who actively pursue comparative analysis without any consideration of the added complexities of the comparative methodology. Øyen suggests that we are all at some point guilty of such behaviour due to the allure of making comparisons to 'others'. The third type of comparative researcher according to Øyen are the *totalists*, or those who are consciously aware of the many stumbling blocks in conducting comparative research but who deliberately choose to ignore them. These could be described as the thoughtful pragmatists of the comparative research world. Finally, *comparativists* acknowledge the above points of view but argue that the advancement of comparative research can only occur through further questioning of its distinctive characteristics. It is the *comparativist* tradition that this book seeks to explore in order to illuminate the distinctive characteristics of comparative analysis within the context of sport and to make more visible the theory and method that underpins it. The comparative methodologist Giovanni Sartori referred to "unconscious thinkers" (Sartori, 1970, p. 1033) as those who undertake (typically quantitative) comparative analysis with little to no recourse to the logic and method of scientific inquiry. In contrast, this book seeks to make those who wish to undertake comparative analysis within the context of sport more conscious of their comparative theoretical and methodological thinking by making the implicit explicit, the invisible visible and the unconscious conscious. In doing so, this book aims to explicate the philosophical, methodological and practical issues of comparing sporting nations and, more broadly, generate further debate and discussion about comparative theory and method within the sport management/policy field.

The ultimate intention of this book is to bring a greater consideration of, and sensitivity towards, the theory and method of comparative analysis for researchers as they prepare for and carry out comparative research. In this manner, and to return to Øyen's typology, this book is advocating for a shift from a *totalist* or pragmatist approach to comparative analysis within sport, towards a more *comparativist* tradition by arguing that sport scholars should be as open and 'conscious' (Sartori, 1970) of their limitations as they are enthusiastic about their findings (Jowell, 1998). It is only once we acknowledge the full extent and nature of the challenges, pitfalls, trade-offs and limitations and become more conscious thinkers when attempting to compare sporting nations, that it will be possible to advance comparative sport research.

The book is written for and designed to be accessible to those who are new to comparative methodology in general and the elite sport policy/management domain specifically. The chapters that follow can be read either in sequential order or separately as required. We recognise the overlap of both the content and examples utilised throughout the book. This is, in part, due to the interconnected nature of the philosophical and methodological issues discussed, which do not necessarily divide conveniently or neatly into the manner in which the chapters are presented. For example, it is difficult to discuss issues of equivalence without including a discussion of, and overlapping with, issues of sampling. The repetition of the examples used throughout the book is also due to the fact that there are a limited number of comparative studies within the sport policy/management domain, which on the one hand means that there are only a handful of studies available to draw upon to illustrate the issues identified within the book. On the other hand, the comparative elite sport policy/management domain provides a clear and discernible literature base by which to be able to discuss the philosophical and methodological issues of comparing sporting nations.

We should also acknowledge from the outset what we mean by the term sporting nations. By sporting nations, we specifically refer to comparisons that are made between geo-political boundaries. We also recognize that the term country is more commonly used to denote a particular socio-cultural divide across a geographical region. Where appropropriate, we attempt to use the more precise term, but in general we treat these terms synonymously and interchangeably throughout the book.

Finally, in outlining the scope of this work, it is perhaps worth specifying what this book is *not*. This book is *not* intended to be a 'step-by-step' guide to conducting comparative analysis within sport. While admittedly a tempting and laudable endeavour, any attempt to do so runs the inherent risk of becoming completely consumed within a philosophical quandary regarding whether there can or should be a single (or multiple), universally agreed upon, methodological approach to comparing sporting nations or even indeed, whether it is appropriate to specify an approach at all. Furthermore, outlining a step-by-step approach also runs the risk of falling into more specific methodological debates about which approach to comparing sporting nations should be promoted and preferred over others. Should variable- or case-oriented approaches be privileged, for example, or should we promote qualitative or quantitative approaches to comparative research in sport? Although this book does address some of these distinctions and highlight some of these issues, these debates are often unhelpful. They create false dichotomies of 'us' and 'them' which can ultimately distract from more fundamental and practical issues relating to how it may or may not be possible to meaningfully compare sporting nations. Providing a step-by-step approach would overlook and ignore the richness and plurality of comparative methodology, and as a consequence, inhibit and limit the various ways in which it can be utilised to examine issues within the context of sport.

Furthermore, this book is also *not* intended to be an advanced treatment of comparative research or the theory and method employed by previous studies. There are many excellent textbooks specifically devoted to outlining particular comparative methodologies – some of which attempt to overcome some of the issues identified herein (e.g., Rihoux & Ragin, 2012). Consequently, this book is not likely to be of particular benefit to those more experienced comparative scholars looking to expand their current comparative methodological toolbox. Rather, this book is intended to generate more attention and focus towards the logic of comparative inquiry within sport and the difficulties, challenges, and pitfalls of undergoing comparative analysis within the sporting context.

The book is structured in three parts with a total of seven chapters. Part 1 – *"Why Compare Sporting Nations: Philosophical Assumptions and Theoretical Approaches"* – focuses on the underlying assumptions and theoretical approaches that underpin comparative analysis within sport. Chapter 1 – *'Is it Possible to Compare Apples with Oranges? The Difficulties, Challenges and Limitations of Comparing Sporting Nations'* – outlines the comparative method and the comparative approach in general, discusses the challenges and limitations of comparative analysis, and sets the scene in general for the chapters that follow by providing a conceptual framework of the challenges and limitations of comparative inquiry in sport. Chapter 2 – *'Knowledge Claims and Philosophical Assumptions of Comparing Sporting Nations'* – outlines the different philosophical traditions that inform comparative studies and the various methodological approaches that can be employed by scholars to compare sporting nations. In particular, the chapter serves to highlight the nature and extent of potential knowledge claims that can (or by extension cannot) be made from comparative analysis. Chapter 3 – *'Why*

Compare Sporting Nations? Purpose, Goals and Level of Analysis' – delves deeper into the underlying reasons and motivations behind making comparisons and how to select an appropriate level of analysis.

Part 2 – *"How to Compare Sporting Nations: Methods, Protocol and Practice"* – and chapters 4-6 (*'Selecting Countries', 'Ensuring Construct, Sample and Functional Equivalence', and 'Data Collection, Analysis and Output'*) in particular, focuses on the specific methodological and practical issues faced by comparative researchers when trying to compare sporting nations as well as identifying several potential strategies for overcoming these issues.

The final section, part 3 – *"Deconstructing Comparative Analysis: Common Themes and New Directions"* broadens the discussion once again by unpacking recent developments and identifying common trends and shortcomings within the comparative sport literature. In doing so, Chapter 7 *'Comparative Analysis within Sport: Challenging the Orthodoxy and Avoiding the Doldrums'* challenges the current status quo and provides a number of potential suggestions for how to advance comparative research within sport.

PART 1

WHY COMPARE SPORTING NATIONS —
PHILOSOPHICAL ASSUMPTIONS
AND THEORETICAL APPROACHES

CHAPTER 1

Is It Possible to Compare Apples With Oranges? The Difficulties, Challenges and Limitations of Comparing Sporting Nations

Chapter objectives

- To acknowledge the difficulties, challenges and limitations of conducting comparative analysis in sport;
- To provide a contextual overview of the elite sport policy/management research domain;
- To provide a framework for understanding and interpreting the philosophical, methodological, and practical challenges/limitations of comparative inquiry in sport.

This chapter introduces the reader to the comparative approach and provides some important theoretical and empirical context to the discussion that follows. The chapter begins by outlining the comparative method and highlights the difficulties, challenges and limitations of comparative analysis in general. In assuming no prior knowledge, the next section outlines the empirical context, the elite sport policy/management domain, from which many of the examples used in this book are drawn. The purpose of outlining this particular research domain is not to provide an exhaustive description of research within this area, but to sufficiently set the scene for the reader to be able to understand and interpret the examples and case studies used throughout the book. To reiterate and elaborate further on a comment within the introduction chapter, the elite sport policy/ management domain is drawn upon here, in part, due to the authors' own background and interest within elite sport policy/management, but also because it offers a useful context by which to explain many of the issues and debates surrounding comparative inquiry. In this manner, the theory and method of comparative inquiry and its application to sport is given a greater priority and emphasis over the specific empirical setting in which it can be applied. Although the book focuses narrowly on examples drawn from the elite sport policy/management domain, it is argued that the book in general, and many of the issues and ideas contained within it, have much wider applicability to any student or early-career researcher seeking to make comparisons within and across a wide range of sporting contexts.

In addition to providing some necessary precursory background information on the research context from which examples are drawn, the latter part of the chapter examines some of the main philosophical, methodological, and practical issues faced by those who seek to make comparisons within sport. Collectively, the chapter provides a broad theoretical and methodological framework that highlights some of the main philosophical, methodological, and practical issues faced by those who seek to make comparisons within sport. This framework will then be used as a structuring device for the chapters that follow. Before proceeding any further, let us begin with a discussion of the comparative method and why it is so difficult to make comparisons.

THE COMPARATIVE APPROACH – COMPARING APPLES WITH ORANGES

To begin to understand the comparative approach it is useful to reflect upon the commonly used idiom that *it is not possible to compare apples with oranges*. This phrase gets to the core logic of comparative inquiry in that it highlights the potential incommensurability of comparing two items that are in this case typically thought to not be comparable. Hofstede (1998), however, argues that although it may not be possible to compare apples with oranges, as these are different objects, it is possible to compare them under the general category of fruits. He argues that if we examine apples and oranges as fruits (a fruitology if you will), then it is possible to compare them based on availability, price, colour, and vitamin content and so on.

Comparative analysis, then, is fundamentally about identifying both the similarity and differences between social units. Comparativists assume that these social units are sufficiently similar enough to be able to make meaningful comparisons, but at the same time sufficiently different to identify differences between the entities studied. The same fruit analogy does not hold when there is no easily identifiable, higher-order abstraction for the entities under study (for example, a football and a pencil share no higher order abstraction).

What can also be drawn from this analogy and the adoption of a fruitology approach in general is that it is necessary to make inferences and generalisations to make meaningful comparisons. Inferences are a fundamental part of the scientific process and can be understood as "an attempt to infer beyond the immediate data to something broader that is not directly observed" (Della Porta, 2008, p. 199). Comparative researchers employ a range of concepts and methodological apparatus to make comparisons between social units. A central question that underpins comparative analysis is, how do we know that the use of concepts and application of methods in one context is the same in another? In other words, to what extent are the concepts and methodological apparatus equivalent (see chapter 5)? If they are not equivalent, then we are not comparing like-for-like social units. We are not comparing fruits.

As will become apparent in the chapters that follow, establishing equivalency is difficult for several reasons. First, it is often difficult to find similar or 'like-for-like' social units (typically countries) to make comparisons. Second, even if it is possible to identify similar social units, the research is often devoid of sufficient knowledge and understanding of the social/historical context in which it is situated. Furthermore, a common criticism that can be made is that the comparative researcher cannot be separated from their own social context, culture and language, and is at risk of ethnocentrism (Dogan & Pelassy, 1990). Therefore, although comparing fruits may be a logical approach in theory, in practice, there is often a limited selection of fruits available to those that seek to make comparisons. Even if there are potentially suitable fruit candidates to add to your study, it is difficult to identify them as they are likely to be on some remote island that is both geographically and socio-culturally inaccessible.

In short, all social researchers should be careful about making generalisations, but given the particular logic of comparative inquiry, comparative researchers should be especially cautious about making inferences and generalisations beyond the sample employed and the limitations of the study. For those interested in conducting comparative research, it is important to recognise that it requires "research procedures that involve caution in order to yield validity in a more differentiated setting" (Przeworski & Teune, 1966, p. 552). It is for this reason that comparative researchers should be as open about their limitations as they are enthusiastic about their findings (Jowell, 1998). We will return to some of these issues in more detail at a later point in this book.

RECOGNISING THE LIMITATIONS OF COMPARATIVE ANALYSIS

The above discussion should not be taken to suggest that making comparisons is impossible or even implausible. It is possible to compare apples and oranges, but it is important to recognise from the outset that making meaningful comparisons is challenging. This section discusses the challenges, limitations and some of the potential strategies of comparative inquiry. It may seem like an unusual place to begin a discussion of the comparative analysis, but discussing the underlying philosophical assumptions and methodological issues provides a useful basis by which to understand the distinctive characteristics of comparative inquiry. It is therefore important to begin to generate an increasing awareness of the philosophical assumptions that underpin a comparative study, and the methodological and practical issues that a researcher is likely to face when carrying out comparative research. Similarly, it is just as important to be able to sufficiently assess the validity of knowledge claims made by other comparative researchers. It is in this sense that this book seeks to develop more 'conscious thinkers' (Sartori, 1970) that are more closely aligned with the *comparativist* (Øyen, 1990) tradition which acknowledges that the advancement of comparative research can only occur through further questioning of its distinctive characteristics.

Due to the complexity and difficulty of conducting comparative inquiry, it is perhaps unsurprising that many scholars have written extensively about the theory and method of comparative analysis within the sociology and management literature (Dogan & Kazancigil, 1994; Dogan & Pelassy, 1990; Ebbinghaus, 2005; Hantrais, 2009; Harkness, 1999; Jowell, 1998; Kohn, 1987; Landman & Carvalho, 2017; Lijphart, 1971; Øyen, 1990; Ragin, 1987, 2006; Sartori, 1970, 1994; Schuster, 2007). Despite this, there remains a paucity of literature that explores these philosophical and methodological issues within the context of sport (for exceptions see De Bosscher et al., 2015; Dowling et al., 2018; Henry et al., 2020; Houlihan, 1997).

Not only is there little consensus about many of the details regarding how to make comparisons, but different comparative scholars have focused on a wide range of philosophical, methodological and practical issues. For example, some scholars have chosen to focus on the fundamental philosophical debates surrounding comparative inquiry (Henry et al., 2005; Øyen, 1990) whilst others have sought to address more general methodological concerns, such as the unit of analysis employed (Dogan & Pelassy, 1990; Jowell, 1998), or focused on specific methodological issues, such as sampling and selection problems (e.g., Anckar, 2008; Ebbinghaus, 2005). Nonetheless, a reoccurring broader theme across this wide-ranging literature base is the acknowledgement of the challenges and difficulties faced when trying to make meaningful comparisons and the recognition that comparative researchers should be cautious when attempting to make comparisons.

Table 1.1 provides a summary of the main challenges, limitations and strategies that can be identified from the comparative methodology literature. It is important to note that this table is not intended to be an exhaustive list of all challenges, limitations and strategies as doing so would be quite impractical and unfeasible. The table more accurately represents an attempt to provide an outline of the broad contours of debate within and across the comparative methodology literature. In doing so, the table offers a potential framework that can be applied to various contexts, including sport, to better understand and interpret the philosophical, methodological and practical issues of conducting comparative analysis. What follows is a brief overview of these issues and some of the potential strategies that have been proposed to overcome or at least mitigate against them.

Table 1.1: Summary of comparative inquiry challenges, limitations and strategies

Issue	Description	Example authors	Strategies
Philosophical assumptions	The philosophical assumptions that underpin, and knowledge claims sought through, comparative inquiry.	Øyen, 1990; Henry et al., 2005; Landman and Carvalho, 2017.	Explicit articulation of philosophical assumptions and recognitions of the types and limits of knowledge claims.
Purpose/goals	The overall purpose and intended outcomes of making comparisons and recognition of their associated strengths and weaknesses.	Øyen, 1990; Dogan and Pélassy, 1990; Henry et al., 2005; Landman and Carvalho, 2017.	Acknowledge and recognise the limitations of these approaches.
Unit of analysis	Deciding whether to focus on macro-, meso- or micro-level policy-related concerns.	Øyen, 1990; Baistow, 2000; Dogan and Pélassy 1990; Hantrais, 2009; Jowell, 1998, Kohn, 1987; Mills et al. 2006; Ragin, 2014.	Clear articulation and justification of the choice of unit of analysis. Recognise the limits of this methodological decision.
Selecting countries (sample)	Deciding which social units to compare (typically countries) and how many to compare.	Ebbinghaus, 2005; Henry et al., 2005; Hantrais, 2009; Jowell, 1998; Landman and Carvalho, 2017; Lijphart, 1971; Ragin, 2006; 2014.	Acknowledge methodological trade-offs. Strike balance between too few and too many countries. More countries are not necessarily better.
Construct equivalence	Ensuring that the concepts employed measure the same phenomena across cases.	Øyen, 1990, 2004; Hantrais, 2009; Jowell, 1998; Johnson, 1998; Landman and Carvalho, 2017; Przeworski and Teune, 1966; Schuster, 2007; Stagmueller, 2011.	Always translate and pilot test comparative instruments using native speakers.

(continued)

(continued)

Issue	Description	Example authors	Strategies
Sample equivalence	Deciding on which countries to include and why.	Øyen, 1990; Ebbinghaus, 2005; Hantrais, 2009; Jowell, 1998; Kohn, 1987; Schuster, 2007.	Need to recognise full randomisation is not possible. Explicit articulation of case selection/ sample strategy to avoid selection bias and the illusion of random sampling.
Functional equivalence	Ensuring standardised methods, apparatus and procedures.	Øyen, 2004; Dogan and Pélassy, 1990; Ebbinghaus, 2005; Hantrais, 2009; Jowell, 1998; Landman and Carvalho, 2017; Schuster, 2007.	Ideally, standardise all data sets. Avoid using secondary data (where possible) or at least acknowledge limitations of inferences that can be made.
Data collection – access and analysis	The methodological trade-off between selecting variables that sufficiently capture the phenomenon in question versus the number of cases and the feasibility and practicality of data collection.	Øyen, 1990; Ebbinghaus, 2005; Landman and Carvalho, 2017; Lijphart, 1971.	Avoid using too many variables to avoid becoming meaningless. Identify a researcher or research team and develop agreed upon operational protocols.
Data output – presentation and dissemination	A number of practical issues relating to the reliability and validity of data (e.g., ensuring standardised protocol, issues of time-lag, and limitations of single-point data) and the willingness of stakeholders to share sensitive information.	Øyen, 1990; Hantrais, 2009; Landman and Carvalho, 2017; Schuster, 2007.	Use multiple data collection strategies. Keep the period from data collection to publication as short as possible.

Issue	Description	Example authors	Strategies
Data output (interpretation/generalisation)	Practices issues around how data are interpreted, how findings are presented and disseminated, for which audience, and how (if at all) this information is used by decision-makers.	Øyen, 1990; Hantrais, 2009; Landman and Carvalho, 2017; Schuster, 2007.	Avoid oversimplifying presentation of data while acknowledging study limitations to the lay audience. Consider the balance between the demands and the trade-offs of comparative design with useful and usable local data for individual countries.

Adapted from: Dowling et al. (2018)

PHILOSOPHICAL ASSUMPTIONS AND KNOWLEDGE CLAIMS

Understanding the philosophical position and the types of knowledge claims it produces remains an important challenge within the general comparative literature (Landman & Carvalho, 2017; Øyen, 1990). Appreciating the different philosophical traditions enables researchers to identify the underlying philosophical assumptions and limits to knowledge claims that can be made based upon them. This includes the nature of the phenomenon under investigation, the types of research questions/hypothesis asked, the choice of data collection strategies and analysis, and the types of conclusions that can be drawn. With the comparative sport policy domain, these assumptions have led to fundamentally different approaches to examining the development of elite sport systems (Henry et al., 2005). Chapter 2 explores these assumptions and knowledge claims and considers their implications for the methodological approaches adopted. One potential strategy for overcoming many practical or methodological debates is to ensure an explicit articulation of the philosophical assumptions that underpin an inquiry and for comparative researchers to acknowledge the limitations of knowledge claims – although this is rarely done in practice.

PURPOSE/GOALS

Closely linked to the above philosophical acknowledgements is the consideration of the overall purpose and goal of conducting comparative analysis. There are several reasons why someone would seek to make comparisons (Landman & Carvalho, 2017). What is important to note is that different motivations (and underlying philosophical assumptions) will lead to fundamentally different research designs depending on the outcome sought. It is recommended that all comparative studies have an explicit statement of purpose with clear aims and objectives to be able to understand the nature and scope of the investigation (Jowell, 1998; Landman & Carvalho, 2017). Chapter 3 provides a more detailed discussion of the different motivations that underpin comparative inquiry and the implications of these for comparative design. In a similar fashion to the philosophical assumptions, the decisions regarding the overall purpose/goal of research should not be left to the reader to infer and should be presented explicitly within any comparative study.

UNIT OF ANALYSIS

Another key issue in comparative research is the unit of analysis chosen. The issue of selecting an appropriate unit of analysis largely depends on the researcher's beliefs about what is knowable, and how it can be known. These beliefs are, in turn, connected to methodological choices regarding the overall focus of the analysis (Baistow, 2000; Dogan & Pelassy, 1990; Grix, 2010; Hantrais, 2009; Jowell, 1998; Kohn, 1987, 1989; Mills et al., 2006; Øyen, 1990; Ragin, 2014). There have been explicit debates about the selection of the unit of analysis within the elite sport policy/management literature. This is also the focus of chapter 3 which examines the various levels of analysis that can be compared, and chapter 4 which considers whether the nation state is an appropriate social unit to analyse.

SELECTION (SAMPLE)

The selection of cases (or sample) is about deciding which particular unit of analysis to compare (typically a nation state) and how many units to compare (i.e., small-N or large-N comparative studies) with either one, few, or many cases (Landman & Carvalho, 2017). In terms of practical strategies, there remains no hard and fast rule for deciding how many countries it is appropriate to compare (Ebbinghaus, 2005; Ragin, 2014). In reality, neither a large-N or small-N sample is preferred, but rather comparative researchers have to acknowledge the methodological trade-off between the number of countries studied and the level of abstraction (Landman & Carvalho, 2017; Lijphart, 1971). The more countries studied, the more general the findings, while the fewer countries studied, the more context-specific the findings. Issues regarding the research design related to sampling are discussed in chapter 4.

EQUIVALENCE

The issue of equivalence is a central but complex issue that is important for all social scientists, but is of particular importance and relevance to comparative researchers

(Baistow, 2000; Hantrais, 2009; Jowell, 1998; Landman & Carvalho, 2017; Mills et al., 2006; Øyen, 1990, 2004; Schuster, 2007). How do we know that what we are comparing is comparable? How do the instruments and apparatus employed mean the same thing in one context as in the other? As equivalence is so important, a whole chapter (chapter 5) has been devoted to this issue. The chapter focuses on three types of equivalence issues: construct, sample and functional equivalence. Interwoven throughout this discussion is the identification of several potential strategies that can be used to ensure equivalence.

DATA COLLECTION, ANALYSIS AND OUTPUTS

The practical issues of collecting, analysing and presenting data are important as they ensure the validity and reliability of the study. These issues include, but are not limited to: ensuring standardised protocols, issues of time-lag and limitations of using single-point data, the willingness of participants and other stakeholders to share sensitive information, and the involvement of external funding or governmental agencies (Hantrais, 2009; Landman & Carvalho, 2017; Øyen, 1990; Schuster, 2007). Many of these issues are evident within the elite sport policy/management domain and are discussed in detail in chapter 6. There are several potential strategies to overcome or mitigate against these problems, including the use of multiple data collection strategies or data sets, shortening the data collection and analysis period, avoiding oversimplifying the messaging and presentation of data, and full acknowledgement of the study's limitations.

The next section provides a brief overview of the research domain from which many of the examples contained within this book are drawn. It assumes no prior knowledge, as many readers may be new or unfamiliar to the research domain. The remainder of the chapter then delves deeper into the specific challenges and limitations of the comparative inquiry within the sport policy/management domain and in doing so sets the scene for the discussion that follows.

THE ELITE SPORT POLICY/MANAGEMENT DOMAIN – THE GLOBAL SPORTING ARMS RACE

The pursuit of international sporting success has increasingly become a taken-for-granted behaviour across many societies (De Bosscher et al., 2006, 2009; Digel, 2002, 2005; Green & Houlihan, 2005; Houlihan & Green, 2008; Kihl, Slack, & Hinings, 1992; Slack & Hinings, 1994). As a result, many countries, vis-à-vis governments, are investing substantial sums of taxpayer funding to the pursuit of medals – most notably at the Olympic and Paralympic Games (Beacom & Brittain, 2016; De Bosscher et al., 2006, 2009; Donnelly, 2009; Green & Houlihan, 2005; Green & Oakley, 2001; Grix & Carmichael, 2012). Some scholars have labelled this increasing interest and investment as the '*global sporting arms race*' phenomenon (De Bosscher et al., 2006; Oakley & Green, 2001).

The image of an arms race of sport performance evokes George Orwell's famous adage that 'sport is war minus the shooting' (Beck, 2013), whereby countries compete for international supremacy with athletes rather than guns to promote their political ideology and superiority on the international stage. One of the consequences of this global sporting arms race is that high performance sport has become increasingly more competitive, complex and uncertain (De Bosscher et al., 2006; Digel, 2002). In response to this uncertainty, many countries have sought, with varying degrees and levels of commitment, to imitate successful predecessors and emulate the successes of the former GDR/Soviet Union in particular (Digel, 2002, 2005; Green & Houlihan, 2005). In discussing the origins of the arms race, Green and Oakley (2001, p. 247) identify that "many antecedents of the former Eastern Bloc's 'managed approach' to elite sport are increasingly apparent" in international sports systems. De Bosscher et al. (2006), amongst other academics, also supports this view by stating "the former eastern bloc countries have undoubtedly played an important role in current developments of elite sport" (p. 194). The GDR/Soviet Union system was considered "the vanguard of developing sporting excellence" (Oakley & Green, 2001, p. 247) due to its consistent approach to producing high performance sporting success. This was not a matter of ad hoc chance or dependent upon uncontrollable environmental factors. Rather, the GDR/Soviet Union model demonstrated international success could be achieved through a deliberate and strategic process of organisational, economic and political calculation (Digel, 2002). The features of this model included a long-term and systematic approach to athlete development, a strong political commitment to support high performance sport, state-controlled apparatus, specialist sport schools/academies, and world-renowned coaching and sport science support (Dennis & Grix, 2012; Green & Houlihan, 2005; Green & Oakley, 2001).

This systematic approach to elite sport performance has been heavily influenced by the broader forces of globalisation, commercialisation and governmentalisation. This in turn, has driven many governments to invest substantial sums of money into pursuing Olympic and Paralympic glory (Green & Houlihan, 2005; Houlihan, 1997). The outcome of this continued pursuit of an 'optimal solution' to winning medals has been an increasing homogenisation or uniformity of elite sport systems, with countries attempting to imitate tried-and-tested methods from others countries through a slow but steady process of lesson learning and policy transfer (Green, 2007; Green & Collins, 2008; Green & Houlihan, 2005; Green & Oakley, 2001; Houlihan & Green, 2008). How and why some nations are more successful than others and to what extent these nations are becoming increasingly similar or different is an empirical question that lends itself to comparative inquiry.

It is against this broader backdrop that the comparative sport policy/management literature has emerged over the past 20 years with academics and practitioners alike seeking potential solutions to a number of increasingly difficult and complex problems in the delivery and management of high performance sport. In particular, comparative sport scholars and practitioners have sought solutions to the following questions:

- How to measure international sporting success?
- What makes some nations more successful at international sport competition than others?
- What exactly do nations need to produce a high performance athlete?
- What is the most efficient and effective way to develop successful high performance athletes?

In response to these general questions, sport scholars have developed extensive comparative research agendas that have produced sophisticated empirical and theoretical accounts of the policy process that characterise the international sporting landscape.

Formative comparative studies of elite sport systems conducted around the turn of the century were largely atheoretical and predominantly focused on providing critical descriptions of elite sport systems (Chalip et al., 1996; Digel, 2005; Digel, 2002; Green & Oakley, 2001; Houlihan, 1997; Petry et al., 2004; Riordan & Jones, 1999). Houlihan (1997) conducted a comparative study of governmental responses to drug abuse and the provision of school sport and physical education in five countries (Australia, Canada, Ireland, the United Kingdom, and the United States of America) utilising a systems-approach and policy community/network perspective. Similarly, Digel (2002), for example, examined the common features and differences of the most successful track and field sporting nations (Australia, China, Germany, France, the United Kingdom, Italy, Russia, and the USA). Digel (2002) identified a number of societal, organisational and societal-organisational relationship factors that influence high performance success. Riordan and colleagues' (Riordan, 1978; Riordan & Jones, 1999) account provides a critical description of elite sport development within communist regimes, identifying specific issues such as talent identification and development, specialist sport schools, integrated sport science and medical support. Chalip et al. (1996) provide a descriptive account of elite sport development in 17 countries. Green and Oakley (2001) investigate emerging trends towards uniformity of elite sport systems. Their analysis revealed 10 similarities in systemic characteristics in approaches to elite sport in six countries (the United Kingdom, Canada, the USA, Australia, France, and Spain).

A second set of comparative elite sport development studies which attempted to go beyond descriptive accounts to provide more theoretically informed comparative research designs began to emerge. Green and Houlihan (2005), examined policy change across three countries (Australia, Canada and the United Kingdom) and three sports (track and field athletics, sailing and swimming) using a modified version of the advocacy coalition framework (ACF), a theory of policy change and agenda setting proposed by Sabatier and Jenkins-Smith (1993). Green and Houlihan's (2005) analysis identified variability in the manner in which countries prioritised high performance sport, however, there was surprising similarity in the underlying causes or factors that led to a high performance sport emphasis. The work of Green and Houlihan (Green, 2004a, 2004b; Green & Houlihan, 2004, 2005, 2006; Houlihan & Green, 2008) was particularly influential during this period. In particular, they developed theoretically informed explanations of elite sport systems by drawing upon a range of meso-level theories of policy change (Green & Houlihan, 2004), policy learning and transfer (Houlihan et al., 2010), path dependency (Green & Collins, 2008), new public management and governance (Green, 2003), and disciplining and governmentality (Green & Houlihan, 2006). During this time several other large scale comparative case-based studies were also carried out by Andersen and Ronglan (2012) and Bergsgard et al. (2007) which adopted theoretical concepts such as isomorphism, the process whereby organisations adopt increasingly similar structures, and its associated mechanisms of institutional change: coercive, mimetic and normative (DiMaggio & Powell, 1983) and other neo-institutional explanations of change to explain the similarity and convergence of elite sport policies in Nordic and western nations respectively.

A more recent set of studies by De Bosscher and colleagues have focused on developing causal explanations of the elite sport policy process and explanations of international sporting success (De Bosscher et al., 2006, 2009, 2015; Truyens et al., 2014, 2016). Through the adoption of logic model approaches to understanding elite sport systems, these studies have predominantly focused on the relationship between inputs (funding), throughputs (facilities, scientific support, talent identifcation and development), and outputs (usually medal count or market share).

De Bosscher et al. (2006) developed a theoretical model for comparing the sports policy factors leading to international sporting success (abbreviated as 'SPLISS'). This model identified nine factors (or 'pillars') and over 100 Critical Success Factors (CSFs) that determine international sporting success. This model was then empirically tested in a preliminary study of six nations: Belgium (separated into data for Flanders and Wallonia), Canada, Italy, the Netherlands, Norway, and the United Kingdom (De Bosscher et al., 2009). The SPLISS framework and its success factors were then later refined and the sample expanded to include 15 nations (composed of three of the SPLISS 1.0 nations: Belgium (Wallonia and Flanders), Canada, the Netherlands, and 12 others: Denmark, Estonia, Finland, France, Northern Ireland (UK), Portugal, Spain, Switzerland, South Korea, Japan, Australia, and Brazil (De Bosscher et al., 2015).

More recently, Truyens and colleagues (Truyens et al., 2014, 2016) applied the SPLISS model to a single sport, track and field Athletics, using a resource-based view perspective. De Rycke and De Bosscher (2019) have expanded on previous comparative studies to discuss the social impact of elite sport systems from the ways elite sport is organised, managed and marketed in society, and have begun to identify how these social impacts might be measured.

CHALLENGES AND LIMITATIONS OF COMPARATIVE INQUIRY IN SPORT

Despite the importance of these advancements and merits of their contributions to enhancing understanding of the elite sport systems internationally, it is important to recognise two inter-related shortcomings. First, much like many other research domains, conducting comparative analysis within sport settings remains both limited and challenging. As a result, it is hardly surprising that there have only been a handful of attempts to empirically investigate sport-related issues utilising a comparative approach. Second, most of those who have sought to make comparisons, particularly within the elite sport policy/management domain, have done so with limited explicit discussion or explanation of their philosophical or methodological considerations. This is probably due to the researcher's focus and interest in empirical findings rather than methodology *per se,* and also restrictions of word count within academic outlets such as journal articles. The consequence of these shortcomings is that there have been limited discussions surrounding the philosophical and methodological approaches that underpin comparative inquiry in sport. The framework articulated above should provide a starting point for responding to this shortcoming. The comparative elite sport policy domain, therefore, offers a useful context by which to apply this previously articulated framework to understand the philosophical, methodological and practical challenges of comparing sporting nations. The application of this framework provides further information about the key authors and studies within the elite sport policy/management literature to help familiarise the reader, and also demonstrates the utility of the framework in being able to understand the theory and method of comparative analysis as it applies to sport.

See Table 1.2 for an overview of the application of the framework to the main elite sport policy/management studies discussed previously. See Dowling et al. (2018) for a full elaboration of this framework and its implications for the sport policy/management domain.

Table 1.2: Summary of comparative inquiry challenges, limitations and strategies of main elite sport policy studies

Issue Study Characteristics/Strategies	Digel (2002, 2005)	Houlihan (1997)	Green and Houlihan (2005)	Bergsgard et al. (2007)
Philosophical Assumptions	Not explicitly stated	Post-positivism Critical Realism	Post-positivism Critical Realism	Post-positivism Epistemology not explicitly stated
Purpose/Goals	To analyse the common features and differences in track and field athletics sport systems in eight countries (Australia, China, Germany, France, Italy Russia, UK and USA)	To examine the policy responses to drug abuse and school sport/ physical education in five countries (Australia, UK, USA, Ireland and Canada)	To analyse the process of elite sport policy change in three countries (UK, Canada and Australia)	To identify the characteristics of sport policy in four countries (Canada, England, Germany and Norway)
Unit of Analysis	Meso and macro level	Meso and macro level – not possible to separate them	Meso and macro level – not possible to separate them	Meso and macro level – not possible to separate them
Selecting Countries (Sample)	Not explicitly stated but aligns with Most Different System Design (MDSD)	Not explicitly stated but aligns with Most Similar System Design (MSSD) Small-N – 5 countries	Most Similar System Design (MSSD) – selected by researchers Small-N – 3 countries	Most Similar System Design (MSSD) – selected by researchers Small-N – 4 countries

Issue Study Characteristics/ Strategies	Houlihan and Green (2008)	De Bosscher et al. (2008)	Andersen and Ronglan (2012)	De Bosscher et al. (2015)
Philosophical Assumptions	Post-positivism Critical Realism	Positivism Realism	Post-positivism Epistemology not explicitly stated	Positivism Realism
Purpose/ Goals	To examine elite sport policy development in nine countries (China, Japan, Singapore, Germany, France, Poland, Norway, New Zealand, and USA)	To benchmark the sport policy factors leading to international sporting success in six countries – experimental pilot study	To examine the similarities and differences of elite sport development in four Nordic countries (Norway, Sweden, Finland, Denmark)	To better understand which (and how) sport policies lead to international sporting success in 13 nations and 3 regions
Unit of Analysis	Meso and macro level – not possible to separate them	Meso – as this is the only level in control of decision/ policy makers – causal modelling	Meso and macro – not appropriate to separate them – focuses on inter-organisational arrangements	Meso – as this is the only level in control of decision/policy makers – causal modelling
Selecting Countries (Sample)	Most Similar System Design (MSSD) – selected by researchers Small-N – 9 countries	Not explicitly stated – pragmatically selected by researchers Small-N – 6 countries	Most Similar System Design (MSSD) – geographically based Small-N – 4 countries	Not explicitly stated – any nation interested invited to participate Small-N – 15 countries and 3 regions

(continued)

(continued)

Issue Study Characteristics/ Strategies	Digel (2002, 2005)	Houlihan (1997)	Green and Houlihan (2005)	Bergsgard et al. (2007)
Construct Equivalence	Not explicitly discussed Analytical response based on interviews, literature review, and document analysis	Not explicitly discussed Analytical response based on secondary data sources	English only – construct equivalence assumed Semi-structured interviews and document analysis carried out by two co-authors Advocacy coalition framework employed	Not explicitly discussed Literature review, document analysis, and 22 semi-structured interviews Analytical framework employed – multiple dimensions: welfare regimes, institutionalism, the advocacy coalition framework, and network analysis
Sample Equivalence	Inclusion based upon medal success outcome (i.e., top 8)	Not explicitly discussed	Explicit statement of sample inclusion criteria: sporting culture, elite sport structures, interest group activity and mature economy	Explicit statement of sample inclusion criteria: economic development, wealth and population

Issue Study Char- acteristics/ Strategies	Houlihan and Green (2008)	De Bosscher et al. (2008)	Andersen and Ronglan (2012)	De Bosscher et al. (2015)
Construct Equivalence	Not explicitly discussed Analytical review in response to Green and Houlihan's (2005) findings by 16 co-authors Analytical framework employed	Translated into five languages (English, French, Dutch, Norwegian, and Italian) Mixed methods – inventory and surveys Econometric and rationalist approach employed	Not explicitly discussed. Semi-structured interviews and document analysis (historical and policy documentation) Institutional entrepreneurship perspective employed	Translated into 12 languages Mixed methods – inventory and surveys Econometric and rationalist approach employed
Sample Equivalence	Explicit statement of sample inclusion criteria: history of Olympic success, government involvement and different socio-demographic characteristics	Sample based upon pre-existing research groups and invited nations	Geographical sample Countries similar in terms of size, socio-economic and political institutions, and strong welfare states	Any nation interested was invited to participate Sample represented 8.5% of world population and 10% global wealth, 23% of total medals at London 2012

(continued)

(continued)

Issue Study Characteristics/ Strategies	Digel (2002, 2005)	Houlihan (1997)	Green and Houlihan (2005)	Bergsgard et al. (2007)
Functional Equivalence	No measures evident from review	No measures evident from review	No measures evident from review	No measures evident from review
Data Collection – Access and Analysis	Predominantly focuses on structural similarities and differences, social conditions, system features and system-environment relationships	Focuses on administrative structure, patterns of government involvement and local and national level	Four policy areas: facility development, full-time athlete support, coaching and sport science and competition	Focuses on analytical dimensions of welfare/ state systems, structure, executive-legislative relations and coalitions.
Data Output – Presentation and Dissemination	Predominantly utilises secondary data sources	Predominantly utilises secondary data sources	2 year data collection period Data collected by authors	1 year data collection period Data collected by authors

Issue Study Characteristics/ Strategies	Houlihan and Green (2008)	De Bosscher et al. (2008)	Andersen and Ronglan (2012)	De Bosscher et al. (2015)
Functional Equivalence	No measures evident from review	European Social Survey (2002) used to measure participation Triangulation of data instruments used	No measures evident from review	Used International Social Survey Programme (ISSP) and Eurobarometer (EB) surveys to standardise sport participation Data excluded if deemed non-equivalent
Data Collection – Access and Analysis	Four policy areas: facilities, full-time athletes, coaching and sport science and competition	Nine policy areas (pillars) 105 critical success factors Established modus operandi	No specific areas identified – institutional theory constructs employed (e.g., legitimacy, isomorphism, organisational field etc.)	Nine policy areas (pillars) 96 critical success factors and 750 sub-factors Established modus operandi
Data Output – Presentation and Dissemination	No empirical data collected	2 year data collection period Data collected by local researchers	Empirical data derived from a number of studies – data collection period(s) not explicitly stated Data collected by local researchers	3 year data collection period Data collected by 58 researchers and 22 policy makers

(continued)

(continued)

Issue Study Characteristics/ Strategies	Digel (2002, 2005)	Houlihan (1997)	Green and Houlihan (2005)	Bergsgard et al. (2007)
Data Output – Interpretation/Generalisation	General conclusion statements	General conclusion statements in response to hypothesis statements regarding similarity of response to issues and the identification of policy communities	General conclusion statements Acknowledged non-representativeness of sample	General conclusion statements – commercialisation and governmentalisation.
	Houlihan and Green (2008)	**De Bosscher et al. (2008)**	**Andersen and Ronglan (2012)**	**De Bosscher et al. (2015)**
	General conclusion statements	General conclusion statements in response to hypothesis statements regarding similarity of response to issues and the identification of policy communities	General conclusion statements Acknowledged non-representativeness of sample	General conclusion statements – commercialisation and governmentalisation.

CHAPTER SUMMARY

This chapter began by introducing the logic of the comparative approach through the analogy of apples and oranges. In response to the question posed in the title of this chapter, it is evident from the above discussion that it is indeed possible to compare apples with oranges, however, comparative analysis is based upon attempts to compare both similar-enough social units so that meaningful comparisons (i.e., similarities and differences) can be identified. The latter part of the chapter provided an overview of the empirical context from which many of the examples contained within this book are drawn. The chapter also sought to highlight the extent of the challenge that lies ahead for those seeking to make comparisons. Comparative analysis is challenging and anyone attempting to conduct a comparative inquiry should be as enthusiastic about their limitations as they are about their findings (Jowell, 1998). In following this tradition, this chapter has presented a framework for understanding the philosophical, methodological and practical challenges of comparative analysis in general and has demonstrated how this can be applied to the elite sport policy/management domain. This framework will provide the basis for structuring the chapters that follow.

CASE STUDY 1: COMPARING APPLES WITH ORANGES – MAKING IMPERFECT COMPARISONS IN PARALYMPIC ELITE SPORT POLICY (DOWLING ET AL., 2017)

In their paper focused on comparative Paralympic sport policy research, Dowling et al. (2017) begin their analysis with attention on the global sporting arms race and an overview of the most common approaches that have been used to compare elite sport systems. Their attention to the global sporting arms race underlines how increased funding and deliberate strategic processes, inspired by the former GDR and Soviet Union, have created a more competitive, complex, and uncertain elite sport landscape (De Bosscher et al., 2006; Digel, 2002). Consequently, academic and practitioner interest in elite sport policy has focused on comparing national sport systems in order to identify critical success factors and how countries may improve performance against these factors in order to enhance effectiveness and cultivate more successful elite sport systems.

The dominant theoretical approaches comparing elite sport systems can be grouped into three categories: the descriptive, the analytical and the variable-oriented approaches. The descriptive approach tends toward an examination of the common features and differences in the sport system. For example, Digel (2002) studied the homogenous and heterogenous features of Olympic sport in eight countries (Australia, China, Germany, France, the United Kingdom, Italy, Russia and the USA), and emphasised the importance of the socio-political context in shaping the elite sport environment in each nation. The analytical approach focuses more on the use of analytical frameworks and models to examine how key elements of the policy process interact, the relationship that these factors share with the environment, and the outcomes that result. Here, Green and Houlihan's work has been important in demonstrating how such models can illuminate the elite sport landscape. For example, in their 2005 paper, Green and Houlihan utilised the advocacy coalition framework to examine the elite sport policy system in Australia, Canada and the UK. The variable-oriented approach utilises mixed methods to assess and compare each nations' performance against nine policy areas (pillars) and over 100 critical success factors. De Bosscher and colleagues (2006, 2009, 2010, 2015) have led the charge on the variable-oriented approach through the development of their theoretical model for comparing sport policy factors that lead to international sporting success (SPLISS). While the SPLISS model acknowledges that macro and micro aspects influence elite sport, the study focuses on nine pillars at the meso level (financial support, organisation and structure, participation, talent identification and development, athlete support, training, coaching, competition and research), as De Bosscher and colleagues contend that these are the only elements that decision-makers can influence.

To date, these models have primarily been applied to westernised nations that are resource-rich. Additionally, the models have exclusively been applied to able-bodied sport. In examining the disabled-sport and Parasport context, Dowling and colleagues (2017) identify five considerations to guide future comparative research in Parasport:

(i) Macro-level considerations: The governance and development of Paralympic sport relates to wider concerns of disability advocacy and culture. Thus, there is a need to examine macro-level social, political and economic factors and the way in which these factors have historically shaped the development of Parasport.

(ii) Comparing by resources: The sharp contrast in levels of support for the development of Paralympic sports between resource-poor and resource-rich countries has resulted in a "gulf in resourcing Parasport" (Beacom & Brittain, 2016, p. 273). Thus, comparing resource-rich with resource-poor countries in a Paralympic context is problematic given the far-reaching structural differences that exist.

(iii) The challenge of construct equivalence: There are clearly marked cultural differences in perceptions as to what constitutes disability and what are considered appropriate social responses to disability. Consequently, construct equivalence is likely to be of equal, if not greater, concern when comparatively examining the Paralympic context.

(iv) The challenge of functional equivalence: There are likely to be fewer publicly available national datasets of disability sport participation. Furthermore, if they do exist, there is still no guarantee that they will be functionally equivalent to enable meaningful comparison.

(v) Accessing data: As the Paralympic system is significantly smaller than its able-bodied counterpart, there are fewer people to contact and collect data from. A further challenge is the dissipated nature of the Paralympic sport system. Additionally, reference to a system itself may actually suggest greater strategic and operational integration than is actually found in many national contexts.

In reflecting on these characteristics, Dowling and colleagues identify two potential paths for researchers seeking to compare Paralympic systems. The first is to apply pre-existing models and pre-determined factors. While researchers can be explicit about the limitations of such approaches, the stated limitations are fundamental as they relate to overlooking or ignoring entirely the very characteristics that make Paralympic sports distinctive and unique from their able-bodied counterparts. A second approach recognises the layers of complexity within Parasport. This approach encapsulates the broader macro-level societal and historical factors that influence the development of Parasport. While this approach has significant value, it requires that researchers move away from "seeking uniformity among variety to studying the preservation of enclaves of uniqueness amongst growing homogeneity and uniformity" (Sztompka, 1988, p. 215). A reasonable starting point, given the paucity of research on Parasport, would be descriptive analysis and classification before advancing into hypothesis testing and prediction.

CHAPTER 2

Knowledge Claims and Philosophical Assumptions of Comparing Sporting Nations

Chapter objectives

- To outline the main philosophical assumptions and knowledge claims that underpin comparative inquiry in sport;
- To understand how underlying philosophical assumptions inform comparative research designs and specific methodological choices;
- To appreciate the general research strategies and methodological approaches that can be employed to make comparisons.

Comparative research in general and all attempts to compare sporting nations are underpinned by philosophical assumptions and knowledge claims. This chapter discusses these philosophical assumptions and their associated knowledge claims in relation to how they inform comparative analysis within sport. As mentioned in the introductory chapter of this book, it is important to recognise all philosophical perspectives and methodological approaches equally. Word count precludes an in-depth discussion of these issues here, however, comprehensive examination of the philosophical assumptions and knowledge claims that underpin social inquiry can be acquired from other sources (e.g., Bryman, 2015; Creswell & Creswell, 2018; Lincoln & Guba, 1985; Patton, 2002). This chapter draws heavily upon Grix (2010) and Creswell and Creswell (2018), as the former provides a comprehensive overview of the research process (see Figure 2.1) and the latter a useful starting point for "assessing the general philosophical ideas behind the inquiry to the detailed data collection and analysis procedures" (Creswell & Creswell, 2018, p. 3) (see Figure 2.2). Combined these insights provide a useful basis by which to discuss the knowledge claims, philosophical assumptions and associated methodological strategies that underpin comparative analysis within sport.

Put simply, knowledge claims are what the comparative researcher claims to be true. As will become apparent in the discussion that follows, what constitutes 'truth' is both a philosophical and methodological concern. All research is underpinned by philosophical assumptions about what can be known (*ontology*) and how we can know something (*epistemology*). Put another way, ontology refers to what constitutes social reality (i.e., what is out there) and epistemology refers to how can we know about it (Bryman, 2015).

Collectively, philosophical assumptions and beliefs are often referred to as a *paradigm*. A researchers' paradigm, or worldview, dictates their perspective on the nature of reality, what is worth studying, what relationships exist to study and ultimately what constitutes legitimate research inquiry (Guba & Lincoln, 1994). For Kuhn (1970), a paradigm is:

> a set of values and techniques which is shared by members of a scientific community, which acts as a guide or map, dictating the kinds of problems scientists should address and the types of explanations that are acceptable to them (p. 175).

Similarly, Senge (1990) defines research paradigms as "deeply ingrained assumptions and generalizations that influence how people see the world or behave" (p. 8). Why, then, is it necessary to begin a journey of how to compare sporting nations with a discussion of knowledge claims and philosophical assumptions? Why is it important to understand a researcher's philosophical *worldview* (or paradigm) when either carrying out comparisons of different sporting contexts ourselves or when trying to evaluate the claims of comparative studies?

First, understanding one's philosophical assumptions and knowledge claims is important for any social scientist, but it is especially important for comparative researchers as they seek to make (often quite bold) inferences and generalisations about social phenomena across nations. Understanding the philosophical assumptions and knowledge claims of comparative research is therefore necessary to be able to appreciate why researchers have designed their study in a particular way and also to be able to effectively evaluate the types of knowledge claims that are being made by comparative researchers.

Second, it is important to understand philosophical assumptions as they inform the methodological choices and decisions that can be made by a comparative researcher. As presented in Figure 2.1, Grix (2010) identifies this as the directional flow of the research process. This process proposes that ontological, epistemological, methodological, methods and sources (data collection) are interrelated and should logically flow from one level to another.

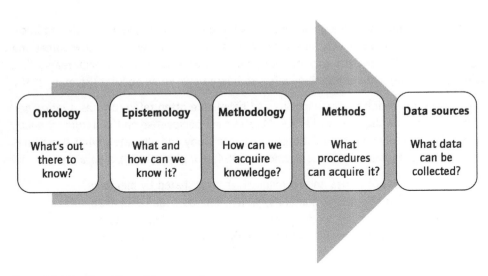

Figure 2.1: Directional flow of the research process
Adapted from: Grix (2010)

Many similar frameworks have been proposed (e.g., Bryman, 2015; Creswell & Creswell, 2018; Crotty, 1998; Guba & Lincoln, 1994; Lincoln & Guba, 1985; Mayan, 2009; Patton, 2002). Crotty (1998), for example, recommends researchers consider: epistemology (theory of knowledge embedded in theoretical perspective); theoretical perspective (philosophical stance informs methodology); methodology (strategy or plan of action that links to methods); and methods (techniques and procedures used to collect data). Similarly, Guba and Lincoln (1994) suggest that three questions need to be satisfied to understand a researcher's paradigm: what is the form or nature of reality (ontology), what constitutes acceptable belief about knowledge, i.e., what can be known (epistemology), and how can the researcher find out what can be known (methodology).

What is consistent between the abovementioned approaches is the recognition of the inter-relatedness of different levels of the research process. All levels of the process, from broad philosophical assumptions about the world to more practical decisions regarding which methods to employ to collect data, are inter-connected. The decision made by the researcher at one level should inform the next. It is for this reason that some scholars have referred to this as the methodological logic or coherence of a study (Mayan, 2009).

A third reason it is necessary to understand the philosophical assumptions that underpin comparative analysis is to avoid false dichotomies regarding knowledge claims. Varying philosophical assumptions can lead to fundamentally different methodological approaches and research outcomes. What can be known in one paradigm, differs from what can be known in another. In other words, 'truth' is relative. Researchers often disagree about the best approach for comparing sporting nations. Many debates that arise within comparative research can be attributed to fundamental differences in underlying philosophical assumptions about how they see the world and how it may or may not be possible to study it, rather than any conceptual or theoretical disagreements per se. For this reason, it is important that researchers be open and explicit with regards to philosophical assumptions in order to avoid the pitfall of "talking past one another" (Grix, 2010, p. 176). This issue is particularly evident within the comparative sport domain, with many of the debates surrounding the best approach to compare nations stemming from more fundamental philosophical disagreements about how to carry out comparative analysis (see case study 6 as an example of how differences in researchers' philosophical assumptions have produced different methodological approaches to comparing elite sport systems). Fourth, and linked to the previous point, clarification of knowledge claims and underlying assumptions is important as it ensures that the researcher can reflexively recognise the strengths and limitations of their philosophical paradigm relative to others (Grix, 2010).

In short, understanding a researcher's paradigm and associated knowledge claims remains an important (if not central) challenge within comparative analysis (Landman & Carvalho, 2017; Øyen, 1990), and the comparative sport policy/management domain specifically (Dowling et al., 2018; Henry et al., 2005). According to Henry et al. (2005), understanding "such [philosophical] issues are of fundamental importance because they are crucial to what we can and cannot know about policy, what different methods can and cannot tell us, and how different claims to policy knowledge might be valid" (p. 481).

At this point, it suffices to acknowledge and appreciate that the philosophical assumptions that underpin comparative analysis should inform the methodological choices and the types of knowledge claims that can be made by comparative researchers. In the next section, we discuss the philosophical assumptions that underpin their research and types of knowledge claims that comparative researchers subsequently make. The remainder of the chapter then focuses on how these assumptions inform the methodological choices available to researchers in order to make comparisons.

KNOWLEDGE CLAIMS AND PHILOSOPHICAL ASSUMPTIONS

We begin by outlining the main philosophical traditions within comparative analysis, an overview of which can be found in Figure 2.2 below. Each of these traditions and their associated claims to knowledge will be discussed in turn.

Figure 2.2: Main philosophical traditions and knowledge claims

Positivism	Interpretivist
• Foundational (realist) • Seeks causal mechanisms • Seeks objectivity (neutrality) • Variable-oriented • Empirical observation and measurement • Theory testing	• Anti-foundational (relativist) • Seeks understanding/meaning • Knowledge socially constructed • Case-oriented • Non-observable and observable phenomena • Theory generation
Post-positivism	**Pragmatism**
• Foundational (realist) • Knowledge fallible (critical) and constantly revised • Seeks underlying generative mechanisms • Stratified reality (real, actual, empirical) • Non-observable/observable phenomenon	• Not committed to a particular philosophical tradition • Problem-centred approach • Seeks problems to solutions • Pluralistic use of methods • Non-observable and observable phenomena • Real-world practice-oriented

Adapted from: Creswell and Creswell (2018); Grix (2010)

POSITIVISM

Positivist assumptions and claims to knowledge have traditionally dominated science and are commonly associated with the 'scientific method'. The scientific method is an approach to research which has characterised the scientific community since the 17th century Enlightenment. This approach often involves the generation of a hypothesis which is either accepted or rejected based on observation, measurement and experimentation through empirical testing (Popper, 1963). The principles of the scientific method are most apparent within the natural sciences, from the simplest of experiments, such as dropping a feather and a hammer off a building to see which lands first, to more complex endeavours like attempting to split an atom using a particle accelerator, such as the Large Hadron Collider – ironically, the largest scientific instrument ever built. Sport-related examples include a VO_2 max test or the testing of artificial stimulants to detect performance-enhancing benefits. Such studies are typically conducted in controlled laboratory settings.

The positivist tradition underscores ideas about how science 'works' or what scientists 'do'. It is the process that we are taught in science class at school. For positivists, the world exists independently from the researcher (realism) and the purpose of science is to gain knowledge or facts through empirical observation of the external world. Positivism assumes that knowledge and facts are 'out there' to be discovered and observed. The purpose of research is, therefore, to attempt to investigate patterns or (ir)regularities within observed phenomena and to identify causal mechanisms of how the world works (i.e., x leads to y). Through the identification of these mechanisms, positivists seek to reduce the complexities of the world to theories or laws (universally accepted theories). Positivists typically seek to test these theories through experimental designs and by controlling for variables that may influence the findings. It is for this reason that positivism is often associated with the variable-oriented approach (see below).

Comparative researchers within the positivist tradition assume that the purpose of comparative analysis is to generate and test hypotheses through empirical observation. It is worth noting that the use of the experimental method (at least in its purest sense) is quite rare in comparative analysis, as it is impossible to study countries within such controlled settings (Lijphart, 1971). Nonetheless, many comparative researchers adopt a positivist approach insofar as they seek to compare nations to identify observed patterns (i.e., similarities and differences) that can be explained through causal mechanisms (e.g., variables x and y lead to outcome z). Comparativists within the positivist tradition believe that the ultimate purpose of conducting comparisons is to understand these causal mechanisms in order to reduce the complexities of the observable world to either develop or test theories.

An example of this from the elite sport policy domain is De Bosscher et al. (2006), who developed a framework for explaining elite sport success (i.e., the SPLISS framework). This is a theory which analysed specific input (e.g., financial resources) and throughput variables (e.g., coaching, talent identification, facilities etc.) relative to outputs (e.g., medals won). The SPLISS research consortium then tested this theory through empirical observation using interviews, surveys and secondary data (De Bosscher et al., 2009). Their study aimed to benchmark the sport policy factors leading to international sporting success based on their empirical observations in six countries. In a more recent study, De Bosscher et al. (2019) analysed the investment strategies of 16 countries. Their study employed descriptive statistics and regression analyses of funding data to measure the extent to which the sample nations prioritise their elite sport funding. Here the authors sought to identify whether there is a causal relationship between prioritisation of select sports and international sporting success (measured by market share in this case).

POST-POSITIVISM

Post-positivism is a more recent research tradition that emerged between the 1950s and 1970s in response to the limitations of the traditionally dominant positivist perspective

(Guba & Lincoln, 1994). In particular, post-positivism emerged from the influential works of Karl Popper's scientific verification by falsification (Popper, 1963). Post-positivists maintain the belief that knowledge is acquired from a world that exists independently (i.e., realist), is empirically observable and from which 'objective' data can be collected (Phillips & Burbules, 2000). Nonetheless, they accept that all knowledge is fallible, theory-laden and provisional (hence post-positivist).

For post-positivists, the research process is about making claims and either refining or rejecting them based on the strength or weakness of the available evidence. Unlike positivists, post-positivists believe that evidence is always imperfect and fallible, with researchers not able to 'prove' hypotheses, but rather able to reject them based on falsification. Popper illustrated this through his famous swan analogy in that the claim 'all swans are white' can be refuted based on observing one black swan.

The post-positivist research tradition contrasts the traditional positivist approach by contending that no absolute truth can be 'found.' Research in the post-positivists tradition is not a straightforward linear process whereby research builds upon one another, but rather a cyclical process of steady rejection, reinstatement and refinement (Edwards & Skinner, 2009). Post-positivist researchers seek to discover the underlying generative mechanisms of the world, which are often deeply embedded within society (Bhaskar, 1978). While positivists believe that the focus of inquiry should only be on what can be observed and measured, post-positivists believe that there are underlying generative mechanisms which can be embedded within both the natural and social world. It is for this reason that post-positivists tend to employ a range of methodological approaches to investigate both observable and unobservable phenomena.

Comparative researchers within this tradition seek to discover these underlying generative mechanisms by observing different empirical contexts. They reject the claim that it is possible to establish complete truth in comparative analysis, but rather posit that all theory and knowledge claims are provisional (i.e., the best estimates based on the available evidence). The purpose of comparative analysis for post-positivists is to seek to identify these underlying generative mechanisms and continually refine knowledge about different contexts. Importantly, post-positivist comparativists reject the notion of relativity and incommensurability adopted by interpretivism. They also reject the notion that we cannot understand the social world due to the socio-cultural differences between different countries. Given their interest in both the natural and social world, post-positivists tend to focus on more in-depth case-study approaches as this enables the researcher to reveal different layers of truth and the underlying generative mechanisms.

An example of the post-positivist approach from the elite sport policy literature is Green and Houlihan's (2005) comparative study of elite sport policies and priorities. In adopting a post-positivist perspective, the authors seek to identify the underlying mechanisms of elite sport policy change in three sports (track and field athletics, swimming and sailing) across three countries (the United Kingdom, Canada and Australia). In adopting a critical-realist approach (a particular form of post-positivism) and the application of a theoretical framework (advocacy coalition framework), the authors sought to explain policy change within these three countries at multiple levels of analysis through in-depth interviews and documentation. In contrast to more positivistic explanations that favour rationalistic and structural views of sport policy (e.g., De Bosscher et al., 2006), Green and Houlihan (2005) – and in their follow-up study of nine countries (Houlihan & Green, 2008) – sought to identify the generative mechanisms leading to the development of elite sport systems. The authors found that there appeared to be common mechanisms and pressures for convergence of elite sport systems, though paradoxically, countries attempt to demonstrate their uniqueness with increasingly similar approaches to developing elite athletes.

INTERPRETIVISM

An alternative approach to positivism is the interpretivism (or constructionism) approach. This paradigm argues that knowledge is socially constructed by humans through their social interactions within the world around them. Interpretivism assumes that "individuals seek understanding of the world with which they live and work" (Creswell & Creswell, 2018, p. 8). For interpretivists, meaning is negotiated between human actors as they go about their everyday lives. These ideas are often associated with the works of Berger and Luckman's (1966) *Social Construction of Reality* and Lincoln and Guba's (1985) *Naturalistic Inquiry*. The former argues people create concepts and mental representations of the social world that over time become institutionalised, or taken for granted, as objective reality within society. The latter outlines a framework for studying people in their everyday lives or 'naturalistic' environment.

As knowledge is socially constructed, interpretivists reject the notion that reality can be understood independently from the researcher. Within the interpretivist paradigm, the production of knowledge is contingent on historical and social contexts. This anti-foundational position argues that truth and knowledge are relative (i.e., relativism). It is for this reason that the researcher's own involvement in the research process is often acknowledged within this perspective, as it is not possible to separate their experiences and prejudices from the research process. In contrast to positivism, interpretivists embrace subjectivity and bias within their research. Interpretivists focus on the lived experiences of participants to understand how their subjective meaning is socially constructed and focus on both the observable and unobservable social interactions within society. For this reason, the approach is associated with qualitative research approaches (e.g., ethnography, interviews and open-ended surveys) and often adopts an inductive approach to generate theory.

The purpose of comparative analysis for researchers within the interpretivist approach is to uncover the everyday experiences of individuals and social units within societies. All experiences are dependent on distinctive historical and social contexts. An extreme interpretivist view, therefore, might suggest that comparisons between nations are simply not possible as they are contextually dependent. Each nation has its very own specific historical and social context and therefore the comparisons are meaningless. For those that do adopt an interpretivist approach to comparative analysis, they often examine a small number or sub-set of cases (small-N) and adopt a range of qualitative methods in an attempt to produce in-depth, intensive and 'thick descriptions' (Geertz, 1973) of particular cases and the social contexts within and surrounding them.

Examples of the interpretivist approach are rare within the elite sport policy/management domain. Perhaps the closest example of this approach is Andersen and Ronglan's (2015) study of policy change and institutional entrepreneurship in Nordic elite sport systems. This study is more closely aligned with critical realism, but is anti-foundationalist with a greater emphasis on the role of agency in being able to navigate institutional fields, as well as polictical and social structures. The notable absence of interpretivist approaches within the elite sport policy/management domain may, in part, be due to the dominance of positivist/post-positivist thinking within the sport management/ policy literature in general (Henry et al., 2020). It may also be explained by the nature of comparative inquiry itself, which tends to attract researchers seeking to uncover patterns of similarities and differences across nations, and the premise of such inquiry by definition implies some sort of realist rather than relativist ontology. This is not to imply that interpretivism is somehow incongruent with comparative analysis in sport. To the contrary, adopting an interpretivist approach to comparative analysis in general, and within the sport policy/ management domain in particular, offers a potentially fruitful approach that has yet to be fully explored.

PRAGMATISM

A final alternative approach to knowledge claims is pragmatism. Unlike other research traditions, pragmatists are not committed to a particular philosophical tradition. In this sense, they are flexible in the underlying philosophical beliefs that are adopted, the form of philosophical inquiry very much depends on the research problem. It is for this reason that pragmatism is often described as the problem-centred approach with an emphasis on 'what works, for whom and when' (Patton, 1990). The emphasis within this approach is the problem, rather than the methodological approach adopted. For this reason, a pragmatist might choose to adopt an array of methods to investigate phenomena.

According to Creswell and Creswell (2018): pragmatism is not committed to any one system of philosophy; individual researchers have the freedom of choice; pragmatists do not seek the world as absolute; truth is what works at the time; pragmatists look to the 'what' and 'how' based on intended outcomes; and pragmatists believe that research always occurs within the social, historical and political context surrounding it.

Much like the interpretivist tradition, to date there appear to be few examples of this within the sport management/policy tradition, however, this approach is perhaps more likely to be adopted by more practically-minded researchers or practitioners within governmental agencies, national sport organisations and other stakeholders with a vested interest in understanding particular organisational or policy-related outcomes. The closest example of this within the elite sport policy/management literature is Digel's (2005) comparison of competitive sport systems in track and field athletics. The study analysed the common features and differences in track and field athletics sport systems in eight countries identifying general social conditions, systemic features and system-environment conditions that lead to international success.

STRATEGIES OF INQUIRY – METHODOLOGY, METHOD AND SOURCES

Following an appreciation of the main philosophical assumptions and associated knowledge claims that underpin comparative analysis, it is important to understand how these underlying beliefs and assumptions inform the adoption of more specific methodological approaches. This section outlines three general approaches to comparative inquiry: the experimental, the statistical and the comparative method, and specifically how these approaches respectively inform two particular orientations (or logics): the variable-oriented and the case-oriented data sources. These orientations then influence decisions about the methodological approach.

METHODOLOGY – QUALITATIVE, QUANTITATIVE AND MIXED-METHODS

This section provides a brief overview of the three broad methodologies that guide the execution of the research: quantitative, qualitative and mixed methods. See Table 2.1 for a summary of these approaches. A more detailed explanation of these approaches can be found in research methods texts (e.g., Bryman, 2015; Creswell & Creswell, 2018; Grix, 2010; Leavy, 2017).

Table 2.1: The distinction between qualitative and quantitative approaches

	Quantitative	Qualitative
Focus	Numerical	Experiential
Philosophical assumptions	Positivist-leaning	Interpretivist-leaning
Research questions	How?	Why?
Nature of inquiry	Objective	Subjective
Logic	Deductive	Inductive
Outcome	Focuses on prediction	Focuses on understanding
Sampling and procedures	Large-N randomised samples	Small-N, non-randomised samples
Data sources	Numerical ('hard' data)	Literacy ('soft' data)
Methods	Experiments, surveys	Interviews, focus groups observations
Analysis	Independent/dependent variables	Codes and themes
Generalisability	Generalisable	Generalisable/does not claim generalisability

Adapted from: Grix (2010)

The variable-oriented approach is often associated with quantitative analysis which tends to be focused on data collection through numbers. Quantitative analysis involves the collection of 'hard' data predominately through surveys and questionnaires. The purpose of quantitative analysis is to test theories through empirical observation of phenomena. This is often referred to as deductive reasoning whereby the researchers attempt to go from generalised theory to specific observation. Quantitative analysis often involves the statistical analysis of the significance between the dependent and independent variables to make inferences about observations.

In contrast, case-oriented approaches are often associated with qualitative analysis and the collection of data in the form of words (e.g., speech, text). Qualitative analysis involves the collection of so-called 'soft' data through interviews, questionnaires, observations, documents and a wide range of other approaches to data collection. The purpose of qualitative analysis is to understand and explore the lived experiences and meaning within the social world of a given case. For this reason, qualitative research often involves asking a series of questions or situating the researcher within a social setting to understand the everyday experience of the participant(s). Qualitative researchers often apply inductive reasoning to their analysis by attempting to go from specific to generalisable findings – although there are many ways of generalising qualitative research (Smith, 2018). This is usually done through the generation of codes, themes, or interpretations of findings.

Mixed methods involve the employment of both qualitative and quantitative approaches within the same study. This usually involves the collection of both numerical and written (textual) data, which are then subject to statistical and thematic analysis respectively. Mixed-methods researchers assume that the collective insight yielded from both quantitative and qualitative data is more insightful relative to a single approach, consequently offering a more integrated and holistic explanation of both observed and unobserved phenomena.

These methodological strategies have clear alignment with general research strategies, orientations and the philosophical assumptions that underpin them. For instance, quantitative analysis is often associated with variable-oriented, experimental/statistical research strategies, and guided by positivist philosophical assumptions. Whereas qualitative analysis is often associated with case-oriented, comparative and interpretivist assumptions. With that said, although presented as two distinct traditions, it is important to recognise that this is a false dichotomy and that "qualitative and quantitative approaches should not be viewed as rigid, distinct categories, polar opposites, or dichotomies" (Creswell & Creswell, 2018, p. 3). It is perhaps more useful to view them as on a continuum with qualitative at one end and quantitative at the other. Any study that attempts to incorporate both is a mixed-methods study and placed somewhere in the middle.

Furthermore, a reoccurring theme throughout this chapter and indeed the book is the recognition that all of these methodological strategies should be acknowledged as legitimate forms of scientific inquiry that can be used for comparative analysis. All have their respective strengths and limitations.

METHODS – THE EXPERIMENTAL, THE STATISTICAL AND THE COMPARATIVE METHOD

Comparative inquiry is often distinguished from other disciplines due to its methodological approach (Lijphart, 1971). Some scholars have argued that this distinction is unwarranted and that the comparative method is no different other forms of social inquiry (Przeworski & Teune, 1966). The renowned political scientist, Harold Laswell, for example, argued that "for anyone with a scientific approach to political phenomena the idea of an independent comparative method seems redundant because the scientific approach is unavoidably comparative" (Laswell, 1868, p. 3). The suggestion here is that all scientific endeavour is at its core comparative in that any attempt to study phenomena through empirical observation and measurement involves comparison. Many other scholars have supported this viewpoint by equating the comparative approach with the scientific method (Lijphart, 1971).

In contrast, some view the comparative method not as a specific type of method (in a philosophical sense), but as a broad brush strategic approach, that can be distinguished as a "method of discovering empirical relationships among variables, not as a method of measurement" (Lijphart, 1971, p. 683). It is for this reason that the terms comparative *approach* or *analysis* are preferred rather than *method*, as the former recognises the comparative approach as a general area of inquiry rather than a specific method. In sum, three core methods constitute the broad comparative approach: the experimental method, the statistical method – and the rather unhelpfully termed – comparative method.

EXPERIMENTAL METHOD

The experimental method is most commonly used in natural science and some social sciences (e.g., psychology). It typically involves the creation of an artificial setting (e.g., lab) whereby empirical observation and data collection occurs. The emphasis of this approach is variable-oriented, whereby the researcher attempts to control for all potential confounding variables to demonstrate cause and effect by eliminating potential alternate explanations. Experimental designs often involve two groups – one subject to a particular stimulus (experimental group) and the other group who do not receive stimuli (control group). This assumes the basic principle of *ceteris paribus* (meaning all things being equal) and that any observed differences identified between the groups can, therefore, be attributed to the stimuli.

Classic experimental designs are quite rare within social inquiry as only a limited number of social phenomena can be studied in this way. Most (if not all) social interaction does not occur within an artificial laboratory setting, and as such it is not possible to undertake experimental methods in many political and social contexts due to practical and ethical reasons (Lijphart, 1971). The entire purpose of the experimental setting is to deliberately create an artificial setting so that variables can be isolated. This is often difficult (if not impossible) or unethical for most real-life settings. Nonetheless, the experimental method is still considered the strongest and most robust method of comparative inquiry when compared to the statistical and comparative method. The experimental method can be understood as the 'gold standard', but often unachievable/unethical approach to comparative inquiry.

STATISTICAL METHOD

The statistical method is an approximation of the experimental method which involves the mathematical manipulation of empirical data that cannot be done within an experimental setting (Jackman, 1985). This usually involves large data sets, examining many cases, often through survey techniques or other big data sets. The assumption made by the statistical method is that there is a degree of homogeneity between cases that allows for statistical comparisons to be made. Unlike the experimental method, however, the statistical method uses partial variable control through partial correlations – but this is not as strong as the experimental method because "it cannot handle the problem of control as well. It cannot control for all other variables" (Lijphart, 1971, p. 684). It is for this reason that the statistical method is generally considered to be weaker compared to the experimental method – but useful for testing theories which can then be subject to more rigorous investigation. Comparative analysis has been traditionally dominated by large-scale statistical approaches with an emphasis on broadly understanding the factors (or variables) that may influence or impact social behaviour. De Bosscher et al.'s (2008) analysis of absolute and relative medal success is an example of this approach from the elite sport policy/management domain. In this study, the researchers employed a linear regression analysis of socio-economic factors that influence relative medal success. Their analysis reveals the difficulties of quantifying and ranking the performance of nations and the increasing competitiveness of international sport evident by the convergance of market share of medal wins across nations.

COMPARATIVE METHOD

A third approach is the comparative method, not to be confused with the comparative approach. The comparative method follows the same logic of inquiry as the statistical method, save one characteristic. The comparative method involves a smaller number of cases, resulting in a sample that is "too small to permit systematic control by means of partial correlation" (Lijphart, 1971, p. 684). It is for this reason that Lijphart (1971, p. 685) refers to the comparative method as an "imperfect substitute" for the experimental method. While the comparative method focuses on a smaller number of cases than the statistical method, it allows for an in-depth and extensive examination of cases, assuming that these cases are broadly comparable but heterogeneous. The statistical method assumes that all cases are homogenous and therefore when controlling for the number of variables it soon does not have enough cases (e.g., nations, organisations, etc.) to employ appropriate statistical analyses. This is more commonly referred to as 'the too many variables, not enough cases' problem (Ebbinghaus, 2005; Landman & Carvalho, 2017; Lijphart, 1971). See chapter 4 for a more detailed elaboration of this issue. For Lijphart (1971), there is no clear division between the statistical and comparative methods, other than the fact that the former relies upon many cases (i.e., large-N) and the latter on much fewer cases (i.e., small-N). If enough homogenous cases can be identified by the researcher, then it should be possible – at least in theory – to adopt a statistical rather than comparative approach. The comparative method has become increasingly more commonplace in comparative research and is particularly evident within the high performance sport domain with researchers choosing to focus on intensive investigations of a small number of countries (see the case study below).

In summary, it is important to recognise that all three of these approaches can (and have been) applied to investigate phenomenon comparatively in sport-related studies. Although there appears to be a general hierarchical ordering of these approaches – with the experimental method being the preferred method in terms of scientific rigour – this is often impractical or unfeasible within many political or social settings. The adoption of statistical or comparative methods is necessary to study the similarities and differences between social phenomena within many sporting and non-sporting contexts.

Another conclusion to draw from the above discussion is that it is important to recognise that whilst there is considerable overlap between these three general approaches, each respectively has their distinctive strengths and weaknesses. On this basis, it is perhaps more useful to consider them as a continuum with the experimental method at one end and the comparative approach at the other, rather than three distinct approaches to comparative inquiry. The decision of which approach to adopt largely depends on the purpose of the investigation, the phenomenon chosen to be studied, the number of variables included and the number of similar cases available to the researcher.

Finally, the above discussion of these approaches may also imply to the reader that there is a singular logic of comparative inquiry. Whether or not there is a singular logic of comparison remains a point of contention within the comparative methodology literature (Della Porta, 2008; Ebbinghaus, 2005; Landman & Carvalho, 2017; Lijphart, 1971; Øyen 1990; Ragin, 2014; Smelser, 1976). Some scholars, such as Lijphart (1971) and Smelser (1976), for example, have argued that these general approaches adopt the same logical reasoning just with different degrees of control and confidence. In contrast, others such as Ragin and colleagues (Ragin, 2006, 2014; Ragin & Zaret, 1983) have challenged this viewpoint, suggesting that although there may be *shared standards* between them, they represent fundamentally different strategies (or logics) to comparative analysis.

When relating the experimental with the comparative approach, there do appear to be quite different general strategies (or logics) employed with the former focusing on identifying the relationships between variables utilising large data sets within a controlled setting, and the latter emphasising an intensive inquiry of a small number of purposefully selected cases. These different strategies (or logics) are more generally referred to in the comparative methodology literature as 'variable-oriented' and 'case-oriented' approaches. These orientations and their underlying assumptions, relative strengths and weaknesses and methodological implications for comparative inquiry will now be discussed.

SOURCES – CASE-ORIENTED VS. VARIABLE-ORIENTED APPROACHES

Variable-oriented approaches focus on establishing relationships between variables, ideally through the random sampling of a large number of countries using sophisticated, statistical, quantitative data analysis techniques that help reduce and aggregate data to make comparisons. Here statistical techniques are used to control for other variables and to isolate the independent variable to generate law-like generalisations. In contrast, case-oriented approaches focus on understanding the complexities of phemonena through a small number of purposefully selected cases analysed with qualitative techniques. See Table 2.2 for an overview of these approaches. What follows is a more detailed discussion of these characteristics.

Table 2.2: Variable- vs. case-oriented approaches

	Variable-oriented	Case-oriented
Focus/Aims	Establishing relationships between variables	Understanding the complexities of specific contexts
Scope	General, extensive	Holistic, intensive
Case	Anonymous	Complex social unit
Number of cases	Large-N	Small-N
Level of abstraction	High	Low(er)
Unit of analysis	Assumes homogeneity	Assumes heterogeneity
Sampling	Random	Purposeful (or selective)
Objects	Observable, behaviourist (objective)	Unobservable, constructivist (subjective)
Theory	Pre-determined, deductive	Emergent, inductive
Generalisability	Seeks to generalise beyond the case	Limited generalisation beyond cases

The variable-oriented approach predominantly focuses on establishing relationships between variables, whereas the case-oriented approach focuses on understanding the inherent complexities of specific cases. Variable-oriented approaches, therefore, tend to favour generality over specificity, placing more emphasis on identifying general patterns of cause and effect. In contrast, the case-oriented approach seeks to understand each social unit (i.e., case) individually, emphasising a level of specificity that requires an intensive and holistic approach to inquiry.

The two approaches also tend to differ in terms of the definition and deployment of *cases* when attempting to make comparisons. The variable-oriented approach assumes that all cases should be treated as the same (i.e., homogenous) and because of their interest in observed effects or patterns across cases, all cases are treated anonymously. Those that seek to establish relationships between variables are subject to the usual principles of statistics in that they need statistical power and certain degrees of freedom. Consequently, the number of cases should reflect the number of variables being operationalised. If there are too many variables for the number of cases, then this can produce what is known as an *indeterminant research design,* whereby there are more variables than observations (Ebbinghaus, 2005). The case-oriented approach, in contrast, assumes that each case is contingent on its complex social and political context and therefore cannot be anonymous.

It is for the above reasons that variable-oriented approaches are often associated with a large *number of cases* (large-N), typically 20+ cases – the assumption being that the larger number of cases the better – as this allows claims to statistical significance. In contrast, case-oriented approaches tend to adopt studies which involve a small number of cases (small-N), typically 2 to 19 cases, because the emphasis is on an in-depth and detailed description of a small number of cases. Case-oriented studies therefore often involve a small number of purposefully selected nations to allow for focused (or "thick") comparisons between cases. In recognising the influence of social and political context, case-oriented researchers tend to focus on similar or like-for-like comparisons as it is not possible to compare completely different units. Bergsgard et al.'s (2007) comparative analysis of stability and change in sport policy purposefully selected four countries (Canada, England, Germany and Norway) based upon their similarity of welfare regimes and governmental arrangements. The study was designed to determine the extent to which sport policy within these countries reflect the characteristics of the broader welfare regime, and how sport policy may be affected by key attributes of the domestic political system and transnational influences, such as globalisation and commercialisation (Bergsgard et al., 2007, p. 4). Similarly, Andersen and Ronglan (2012) selected four Nordic countries based on their geographical proximity and similarity of ideology, welfare regimes and governmental and administrative stuctures. The purposeful selection of a small number of cases also leads to a methodological choice between whether to adopt either a most similar, or a most different research design (see chapter 4 for a more detailed discussion of sampling). Case-oriented researchers tend to disagree with the variable-oriented assumption that more cases (i.e., larger-N) are better. This is on the basis that more cases: potentially risk increasing confounding variables; require researchers to utilise concepts that may not have equivalence (sometimes called concept stretching); and run the risk of not being able to gather sufficiently deep enough knowledge of cases (Della Porta, 2008). Equally, variable-oriented researchers would question the validity of case-oriented analyses that employ so few cases, as there is not a sufficient number of cases to develop statistically generated causal effects.

It is because of the large number of cases that variable-oriented approaches tend to focus on higher levels of *abstraction* compared to the case-oriented approach which focuses on a lower level of abstraction. Variable-oriented approaches tend to ignore the complexities of the macro-environment, either because they are unobservable or because of the limited number of variables that can be considered within the analysis. In contrast, case-oriented approaches tend to embrace the macro level of analysis, as it is not possible to separate each case from the broader socio-political context, and therefore any case must be understood within this broader context — see chapter 3 for an in-depth discussion of units of analysis.

A final point of divergence between the two orientations lies in their use of *theory*. Variable-oriented approaches often involve the pre-determined or deductive use of theory, whereby empirical observations are typically used to test these theories to determine whether they reflect observed reality. It is in this sense that variable-oriented approaches are seeking to discover law-like generalisations that are applicable across many (if not all) cases. In contrast, case-oriented approaches emphasise the importance of generating theoretical accounts through inductive approaches. The case-oriented approach, therefore, acknowledges the limited generalisability of findings as they are often context-dependent.

Within the comparative elite sport policy/management literature there appears to be broad alignment between those studies that emphasise the variable-oriented approach. These approaches statistically analyse the relationship between dependent variables (often medal count or market share) and independent variables such as gross domestic product (GDP), population size, and other structural factors. By comparison, those who emphasise a case-oriented approach provide more critically descriptive and theoretical accounts of the policy process in elite sport systems (cf. Bergsgard et al., 2007; De Bosscher et al., 2009). See the case study at the end of this chapter for a detailed account of variable- vs. case-oriented approaches within the elite sport policy/management domain.

CHAPTER SUMMARY

This chapter has sought to outline the philosophical assumptions and knowledge claims that underpin comparative inquiry in sport. Before undertaking comparative analysis, it is necessary to understand the assumptions and limitations of knowledge claims that are being sought by the researcher, and to appreciate the philosophical and theoretical perspectives that underpin the inquiry in order to avoid 'talking past one another' (Grix, 2010) when debating methodological issues. These underlying philosophical assumptions lead to the adoption of a general research strategy. This strategy, in turn, tends to follow either a variable or case-oriented approach to inquiry. Depending on which approach is used, researchers adopt a qualitative, quantitative or mixed-method approach to compare sporting cases. The logical flow of research strategy considerations discussed throughout this chapter are summarised in Figure 2.3. It is equally important to recognise the utility of all approaches that are available to those seeking to make comparisons in sport and it is argued here that no one approach should be favoured over another, as each of these approaches, "has its own set of advantages and disadvantages involving scope of coverage, level of abstraction, ability to use quantitative and qualitative methods, and its ability to draw secure inferences" (Landman & Carvalho, 2017, p. 29). To be clear, it is the plurality of research approaches that allows for a more holistic appreciation and deeper understanding of comparisons within sport.

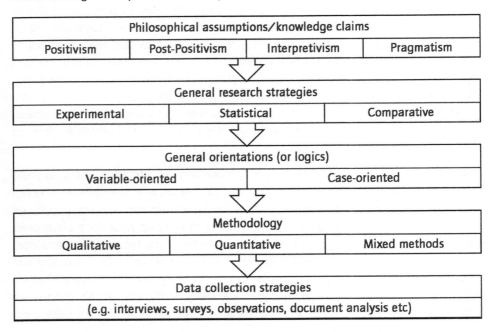

Figure 2.3: Summary of research strategy considerations for comparative analysis

CASE STUDY 2: VARIABLE- VS. CASE-ORIENTED APPROACHES WITHIN ELITE SPORT POLICY/MANAGEMENT

In the previous chapter, we outlined the descriptive, analytical and variable-oriented approaches as being the dominant ways in which elite sport systems are compared. These ways of comparing sport can be further developed to consider two overarching methodologies: the case-oriented and the variable-oriented. Here, the descriptive and analytical approaches are commonly used in the case-oriented methodology, whereas variable-oriented studies are rarely incorporated into a case-oriented approach. This case study seeks to provide an example of each methodology demonstrating the key differences in the purpose, goals and approach typically used in the case-oriented methodology and the variable-oriented methodology.

The case-oriented methodology is most commonly coupled with qualitative techniques, collecting data in the form of words, using instruments such as interviews, questionnaires, observations and documents. The data generated is then typically analysed by generating codes, categories and themes in order to reduce and index the data so that the researcher may make sense of it in relation to their research question (Cresswell, 2018). The purpose of qualitative analysis is to explore the lived experience and constructed reality of a particular phenomenon. As a result, the case-oriented methodology relies upon the researcher(s) being able to situate themselves in the social setting under study in order to explore and understand the everyday experience of the participant(s). The case-based orientation typically relies on inductive reasoning where specific case-based findings may be generalised, with variable degrees of caution, to other social settings.

A practical example of the case-oriented methodology is Bergsgard et al.'s (2007) comparative analysis of stability and change in sport policy. The goal of the study was "to identify the characteristics of sport policy in four countries (Canada, England, Germany and Norway), to determine whether, and to what extent, sport policy reflects the characteristics of the broader welfare regime, and whether, and in what ways, sport policy is affected by key attributes of the domestic political system and transnational influences, such as globalisation and commercialisation (Bergsgard et al., 2007, p. 4). The research design of the study suggests that it is guided by an interpretivist philosophy as the researchers sought to construct a "thick description" of knowledge from secondary sources. More specifically, the study utilised an analytical framework to examine the relationship between structure and agency in its broad cultural and historical setting, particularly in relation to the four major forces that influence national sport policy, namely commercialisation, globalisation, politicisation and governmentalisation (Bergsgard et al., 2007). This addressed a range of social, political and historical factors such as: cultural differences, welfare regimes, state systems, executive-legislative relations, government-interest group relations and dominant interests. In addition, their analysis examined how institutional factors such as administrative arrangements, patterns of resource dependence, interaction between interest groups, the dominant policy paradigm, the sport-specific policy paradigm, and the deep structural values and storylines influenced a range of policy sub-fields such as sport and the voluntary sector, sport for all and high performance sport. In concluding their work, Bergsgard et al. (2007) stress the need for nuanced description and comparative analysis, as permitted by a case-based methodology, as such approaches can expose the broad trends where commercialisation and globalisation underpin convergence in sport policy across nations and, at the same time, reveal where sport policies reflect national political and cultural peculiarities (Bergsgard et al., 2007). In short, the work of Bergsgard and colleagues (and others who work with case-based methodologies) reinforce the importance of context, the very basis of a reality that is socially constructed, and the need to construct thicker descriptions of reality in order to deepen our understanding of the issues under investigation.

The variable-oriented methodology is most commonly paired with quantitative analysis. Quantitative analysis involves the collection of numerical data through surveys and questionnaires. The purpose of quantitative analysis is to test theories through empirical observation of phenomena. This is often referred to as deductive reasoning, whereby the researchers attempt to go from generalised theory to specific observation. Quantitative analysis often involves the statistical analysis of the significance between the dependent and independent variables to make inferences about observations.

De Bosscher's (2009) study of international sporting success is an apposite example of the variable-oriented methodology. The study utilises a pre-existing framework consisting of nine policy pillars (detailed in case 1) to examine international sport success in six countries. The policy pillars, presented as a logic model of inputs and throughputs which lead to certain outputs, were operationalised into 105 critical success factors, which were then translated into specific questions that formed the basis of two survey instruments. The first instrument, the sport policy survey, was completed by the research team in each country. The second instrument, the sport climate survey, was completed by athletes, coaches and performance directors involved in elite sport. Research participants were required to score each question using a five-point scoring scale, where a score of one represented little or no development and a score of five reflected a high level of development. Following this, an overall percentage score for each pillar was calculated by aggregating the data per question together with non-responses. The aggregated data are then presented to show the relative market share or performance of each nation based on their share of the medal wins together with the ratings of each nation against each of the nine pillars. This data then allows for a general discussion of the relationship between inputs (financial support), throughputs (the other pillars) and outputs (medal wins), and a more specific analysis of the drivers of an effective system and the factors that enable nations to develop a competitive advantage.

Clearly, the earlier work of De Bosscher and colleagues (SPLISS 1.0 rather than 2.0) reflects the positivist tradition insofar as the goals of the research are concerned with causal relationships between inputs, throughputs and outputs. The study allows general statements or hypotheses to be accepted or rejected based on the measurement of different scores across nations. At the conceptual level, the study design has the appearance of a more objective research exercise, despite the reality of the subjectivities involved in scoring each critical success factor. Finally, the study demonstrates how the variable-oriented approach permits numerical data to be used to give meaning to a complex and nuanced reality.

CHAPTER 3

Why Compare Sporting Nations? Purpose, Goals and Level of Analysis

Chapter objectives

- To understand the varying motivations that underpin comparative research;
- To appreciate how varying motivations, purposes and goals lead to the adoption of different methodological approaches;
- To describe how motivations, purposes and goals inform the level of analysis selected.

The usage of comparisons is commonplace within society and as social entities, we are constantly seeking to make comparisons between ourselves and others – and sport is no exception. The central question of this chapter is, why then do we decide to make these comparisons? What is the overall purpose or goal of comparing countries? What are the underlying motivations or reasons for comparing countries? What is it that we seek to know and understand through these comparisons? This chapter examines these questions and explores how different motivations underpin comparative inquiry.

The chapter begins by discussing the general reasons why we seek to make comparisons. This is followed by a more specific discussion of the varying goals or purposes of comparative inquiry by drawing upon Landman and Carvalho's (2017) typology of reasons for carrying out comparative research: description, classification, hypothesis and prediction. As will become clear, these varying reasons are inter-related and are linked to the underlying philosophical assumptions and knowledge claims sought. Also, in much the same way as the underlying philosophical assumptions and knowledge claims discussed in the previous chapter, these different motivations often lead to the adoption of different methodological approaches to comparative inquiry. The second section then focuses on the use of theory in comparative research. This is important as there is an inescapable connection between comparisons and theory (Dogan & Pelassy, 1990), and many consider the *raison d'etre* for carrying out comparative inquiry to be to test and generate theory (Dogan & Pelassy, 1990; Landman & Carvalho, 2017;

Lijphart, 1971). The final section begins to set the scene for part 2 of the book, by turning towards methodological concerns relating to how these underlying motivations, goals and purposes inform decisions on which level of analysis to focus in order to make comparisons.

WHY COMPARE? MOTIVATIONS FOR COMPARISON

In response to the question of why we seek to compare and the underlying motivations for making comparisons, researchers will cite a variety of reasons. The most common reason is that it enables social scientists to develop theories about the social world. That is, to be able to understand the underlying mechanisms or general patterns that shape social behaviour. This is the ultimate goal of conducting comparative inquiry – to produce a theory of social behaviour (see discussion below). To understand the various motivations for conducting comparative analysis, it is worth considering why we make comparisons on a more individualistic level, i.e., why one person would want to compare themselves with another.

When asking anyone why they compare themselves with another, the response might be because it enables them to better understand themselves. Gathering a better understanding of ourselves enables us to appreciate the everyday assumptions that underpin our lives. What is it that we take for granted in our everyday lives? The clothes we wear, the way we dress, what we like and dislike, what we value and what we don't value, what is considered 'normal' or 'usual' in both the individual and cultural sense. This is often the typical (albeit clichéd and stereotypical) case for teenagers and young adults to go travelling, for example, in that it helps them 'find themselves' and to 'appreciate better' 'where they are from' and 'what makes them unique' compared to others.

The same principle applies to comparing one country with another – albeit with additional layers of complexity. At the most basic level, comparing one country with another enables us to understand the similarities and differences between countries. Comparing one country with another thus enables us to better understand the differences between societies and cultures. What makes one country unique or different compared to another? Equally, what similarities and patterns are the same across nations? In making these comparisons and by developing a better understanding of other contexts, we are in turn attempting to better understand ourselves. Hence, comparative analysis can be understood as putting up a giant, country-sized, mirror that allows us to see ourselves in both the practical and meta-philosophical sense and to gain knowledge about our own setting. As Dogan and Pelassy (1990, p. 5) rather succinctly put it "knowledge of the self is gained through knowledge of others". Far from a simple data-gathering exercise, comparative analysis:

> Represents a quest for enlightenment. And that is what
> makes it one of the most fruitful ways of thinking. It helps
> us rid of inherited fossilized notions, obliges us to reconsider
> the validity of undiscussed interpretations, and enlarges
> our visual field. In other words, it helps us guard against
> ethnocentrism (Dogan & Pelassy, 1990, p. 9).

In considering motivations in a more theoretical and practical sense, there are a variety of reasons for conducting comparative inquiry. Houlihan (1997, p. 7) identifies three major practical reasons for conducting comparative policy analysis in sport. First, it enables policy-makers to learn from different countries in general and political/sporting systems in particular, to be able to tackle similar problems (e.g., responses to doping). Second, it encourages policy-makers to adopt a broader perspective and help reveal underlying assumptions of current policy options. Third, it helps polticians and decision-makers to avoid cultural-bound generalisations to resolve domestic issues. Similarly, Hantrais (2009) identifies several theoretical and practical reasons for carrying out comparative analysis. Theoretical justifications include providing an empirical basis for the development of theory, the search for explanatory factors or general laws that can explain social phenomena and the verification or falsification of relationships between variables amongst others. More practical reasons for carrying out comparative inquiry include to inform policy, identify common policy goals/objectives, evaluate potential solutions to societal problems, share policy learning, identify best practices and support processes of continuous improvement. These remarks illustrate that there are a variety of reasons for carrying out comparative analysis and these reasons often differ depending on the outcome sought. The underlying reasons for conducting comparative analysis, therefore, lead to quite different approaches to be adopted by researchers, an issue to which we will return.

Many attempts have been made by comparative methodologists and sociologists to distinguish between and classify the different motivations which underpin comparative inquiry (Kohn, 1989; Landman & Carvalho, 2017; Ragin, 2014) and within sport (Henry et al., 2005). In his earlier work, Kohn (1989) identified four main types of comparative research, each driven by a different set of motivations. These four types of studies are known as *object, context, unit of analysis* and *transnational* studies. The primary interest of (i) *object*-based studies is the country under investigation. Here comparative researchers focus on how a country compares to other countries purely in an attempt to better understand itself. Comparative analysts in this tradition want to know about a country for its own sake, rather than as an attempt to generate a general hypothesis or seek to identify underlying patterns. (ii) *Context*-based studies focus on testing the generality of findings beyond a singular context. They seek to identify social patterns across different contexts. Countries are treated as a means to an end in that they enable researchers to identify and generate theory. Kohn (1989), notes that it is often difficult to distinguish object- from context-based comparative studies. (iii) *Unit of analysis* type studies seek to identify the similarities and differences amongst distinct characteristics of countries. In this type of comparative study, the emphasis is on the variables/characteristics under investigation and how particular social units are connected to variations (i.e., similarities and differences) between countries. An example of this from the sporting context is the relationship between gross domestic product (GDP) and elite sport success (medal count). (iv) *Trans-national* comparative research treats countries as a part of a larger component of an international system, e.g., globalisation, capitalism etc. Here the country is almost entirely treated as anonymous with the emphasis on macro-level societal trends. Kohn's (1989) distinction acknowledges the various forms in which comparative studies can take place, noting the specific emphases and the potential to focus on different levels of analysis.

The variety of different approaches to comparative analysis was built upon by Henry et al. (2005) who produced a four-fold typology of comparative sports policy studies. This included: Type 1 – *'Seeking Similarities'*, a nomothetic approach to seeking law-like generalisation. Type 2 – *'Describing Difference'*, an ideographic approach that seeks to capture the specificity of policy systems. Type 3 – *'Theorising the Transnational'*, which goes beyond national borders to examine a combination of local and global factors and Type 4 – *'Defining Discourse'* which focuses on how discourse defines policy problems. The case study at the end of this chapter elaborates further on this typology and its implications for comparative sport scholarship.

Landman and Carvalho (2017) provide a comprehensive and accessible attempt to capture the underlying motivations and their associated outcomes in their typology of reasons for carrying out comparative research. These include four main reasons: description, classification, hypothesis and prediction. *Descriptive* studies involve collecting detailed descriptive accounts of particular national contexts; these are often employed as a starting point for other types of comparative research. *Classification* studies attempt to reduce the complexities of the social world by identifying common features through categorisation and/or the creation of typologies. *Hypothesis* testing studies involve the search and testing of explanatory factors that cause certain social patterns. Finally, *predictive* studies involve predictions about particular causal effects in the social world, based upon generalisations from previous comparisons.

CONTEXTUAL DESCRIPTION

Studies focused on contextual description require as much description and detail about a particular context as possible. The focus of this approach is to provide an in-depth, intensive account of a country through the generation of 'thick description' (Geertz, 1973). It is for this reason that descriptive studies are often associated with the case-study approach (Yin, 2017) which involves the investigation of contemporary phenomenon, in-depth within its real-world context, usually through the multi-method approach to data collection. The intended outcome of this particular type of study is to provide as much detail as possible about a particular setting in an attempt to better understand it. It is often due to the richness and detail of a descriptive study that enables it to be used as the basis for higher-order comparative studies. Examples of this from the elite sport policy/management domain include Digel's (2002) study of the top ten track and field athletics nations (by total medal count). This study centred on a detailed descriptive account of the general social conditions, general features, sport systems and system-environmental factors that explained high performance success. The aim was to provide an in-depth analysis of these nations in an attempt to explain why certain countries were successful at winning medals in successive international competitions.

CLASSIFICATION

Classification studies attempt to reduce complex social realities through the identification of common features through categorisation and the creation of typologies. The purpose of classification studies is to establish conceptual or theoretical lines by which countries can be divided. These can be simple dichotomies (e.g., democratic and autocratic) or more complex matrices or typologies (e.g., Finer's [1971] classifications of government). Unlike descriptive studies, classification studies attempt to identify and utilise underlying conditions in order to create categories into which countries can be grouped. There are few examples of classification across sporting nations, but there are studies that have attempted to classify sport organisations. Kihl et al., (1992), for example, classified national sport organisations as being volunteer-driven based organisations (kitchen table), a combination of volunteers and professionals (boardroom), or increasingly professionalised (executive office) entities. There have been similar attempts to categorise comparative sport studies, such as Henry et al. (2005), who developed a four-fold typology of comparative sport studies each with their associated strengths and weaknesses. This typology and its implication for comparative analysis in sport are discussed in the case study at the end of this chapter. Collectively, these studies can be seen as classification-based studies as they are seeking to reduce complexity through the identification of common features.

HYPOTHESIS TESTING

The development of hypotheses and testing theory is the third reason for pursuing comparative studies. This approach requires a higher-order process as it involves postulating about the relationships between often complex and potentially interacting and intervening variables. For these types of studies, comparative researchers search for factors that explain what has been previously described and classified. The emphasis is on identifying explanatory variables − often through descriptive and classification accounts − proposing potential relationships between factors and then testing these propositions through empirical inquiry to generate theory. This is perhaps the closest thing to the *comparative method* described by Lijphart (1971) and Przeworski and Teune (1970). The SPLISS studies (De Bosscher et al., 2009, 2015) are examples of this type of study within the sport domain whereby the researchers were interested in identifying the factors responsible for international sporting success and then applying them to specific nations.

PREDICTION

The final reason for carrying out comparative analysis is to make predictions. These predictions are usually based upon the generalisations made from previous comparative studies. The aim here is to make predictions from these generalisations that can then be applied to other countries not involved in the study. For this reason, it is considered to be the most difficult and complex of all types of comparative study, in that explanatory factors and variables must be exacting, clearly understood, and supported by empirical evidence so that predictions about future events can be made. Unsurprisingly, there are no examples of this type of comparative study within the sport policy/management literature, but it is this type of study to which most other comparative researchers aspire because it can generate and test theory to be able to predict certain outcomes (Landman & Carvalho, 2017). In many respects, this is the ultimate goal of many elite sport policy/ management comparative studies: to be able to predict who will win the most medals at the Olympic and Paralympic Games based on a complex combination of system design factors. Predictions also do not have to be specific event outcomes, but could be broader societal shifts, such as the shift towards the prioritisation of elite sport in many western nations.

In general, three features can be drawn from Landman and Carvalho's typology. First, that these four different types of comparative studies are not mutually exclusive and are inter-related in that one level informs the next. It is common for descriptive and classification studies to be used as the basis for generating and testing hypotheses or making predictions. In this sense, describing and/or classifying comparative research is an important and necessary precursory step for developing more complex and causal explanations of social phenomena. Second, each of these types of study involves its own set of challenges and limitations. Descriptive studies, for example, produce detailed accounts with the inherent risk of producing too descriptive and arguably non-generalisable accounts. Classification studies, meanwhile, have the potential to reduce the complexities of social reality to the point of becoming meaningless. Hypothesis and prediction studies are also not only difficult, but have the specific challenge of needing to delineate the nature of the relationship between variables. These limitations are often not explicitly acknowledged or discussed by comparative researchers. Third, it is apparent that there is a clear 'hierarchical ordering' between these reasons for conducting comparative research, in that descriptive studies are generally considered to be a 'lower-order' while hypothesis testing and predictive studies are 'higher-order'. Therefore, regardless of what the underlying motivations might be, or the type of comparative study and outcome sought, it is important to keep the ultimate intention of comparative inquiry in mind, that is, to test and generate sociological theory. The next section discusses the important role of theory within comparative inquiry in more detail.

USE OF THEORY IN COMPARATIVE INQUIRY

Perhaps the most important aspect of appreciating why people undertake comparisons is through acknowledging the role and use of theory within comparative research. Before discussing theory, however, it is worth considering the different types of variables and constructs utilised by researchers and how these are used to inform theories. This may seem rudimentary, but it is necessary to be able to understand how theory is employed by comparative researchers and how it underpins comparative inquiry.

Creswell and Creswell (2018) provide a succinct elaboration on the role and use of theory in social research. According to Creswell and Creswell (2018), a variable is a "characteristic or attribute of an individual or an organization that can be measured or observed and that varies among the people or organization observed" (p. 51). A variable, as the name suggests, is a value or measure that can change. There are main two variables: *independent* and *dependent* variables. *Independent* variables "are those that influence or affect outcomes" (Creswell & Creswell, 2018, p. 51). *Dependent* variables "are those that depend on the independent variables, they are outcomes or results of the influence of the independent variables" (*ibid*). An example of this in sport might be the factors that lead to increased participation. The dependent variable usually measured by moderate to highly intensive physical activity is participation over a set period of time (i.e., per week, per month, per year), and the various potential factors that may influence participation (i.e., age, gender, ethnicity, education, household income) are independent variables.

There are two additional types of variables that are particularly relevant for comparative analysis: *control variables* and *compounding variables*. *Control variables* are other independent variables that are known to influence the dependent variable. In comparative research, these are often difficult to account for, and the analysis is often reduced to a country-by-country comparison. *Compounding (or intervening) variables* are variables which mediate between the dependent and independent variables. This is a common concern in comparative analysis, as it is not possible to control for all possible compounding variables in non-artificial, real-life settings. This is why it is very difficult to make any definitive claims about the findings of most comparative studies. A good example of this is De Bosscher et al. (2009) in their pilot study of the development of elite sport nations. In their study involving six nations, the researchers only provided tentative conclusions based on their preliminary findings, as it was not possible to say with any confidence that there were no additional compounding variables that could explain the outcome of elite sport success by medal count (dependent variable). Issues relating to control variables and compounding variables will be discussed in subsequent chapters relating to sampling and equivalence, in chapter 4 and chapter 5 respectively. The studying of the relationship between the dependent and independent variable(s), and making predictions or propositions between them, is a *hypothesis*. When we test hypotheses or propositions across several different contexts we are developing theory.

A theory then is, "an interrelated set of constructs (or variables) formed into propositions, or hypothesis, that specify the relationship among variables (typically in terms of magnitude or direction" (Creswell & Creswell, 2018, p. 52). Theory can be understood quite simply as the organising of concepts aimed at explaining reality. It is an effort at synthesising the causes of observed phenomena and elaborating on sociological rules (Dogan & Pelassy, 1990). Theory is an attempt to simplify or depict social reality. It is a "definitive and logical statement (or groups of statements) about how the world (or some key aspect of the world) 'works'" (Landman & Carvalho, 2017, p. 309).

Landman and Carvalho (2017) distinguish between *normative* and *empirical* theory. *Normative theories* are statements which contain subjective or value-laden judgements about how society *ought* to be, given intended outcomes and philosophical position. *Empirical theories* are factual or objective statements about how society works through establishing relationships between variables.

A comparativist's perspective and use of theory is dependent upon their philosophical viewpoint and research tradition. Creswell and Creswell (2018) elaborate by distinguishing between quantitative and qualitative use of theory and the various ways in which theory is employed within these traditions. This general view on theory can also be called a *theoretical framework* or theoretical lens which provides the overall perspective that informs and helps guide the general direction of a research study – examples of this within elite policy/management sport domain often include public administration and political theory (e.g., policy change, governance), organisational theory (e.g., resource-based view, institutional theory), or sociological perspectives (e.g., Foucauldian, figurational, relational).

All comparative researchers believe that the comparative approach is the only means by which to make an empirical observation about the social world, as the experimental method is either impractical or unethical in the 'real-world'. For this reason, the comparative approach is the only means by which to elaborate on and find these so-called sociological rules (Dogan & Pelassy, 1990). The statements of theory or sociological rules can be generated and tested through the systematic use of comparative methods. As this is the only means by which to make these systematic empirical observations of social reality, comparative researchers must start with a theoretical foundation or base, otherwise they cannot make meaningful comparisons as they do not know what to look for. For Landman and Carvalho (2017, p. 291), "careful theorizing about political events and political outcomes will lead scholars to compare similar outcomes in different cases or different outcomes in similar cases"– depending on the design employed (see chapter 4 on sampling and most similar system and most different system designs). Landman and Carvalho (2017) conclude that:

> Comparativists ought to spend more time on careful theorizing and research design. Once the assumptions of theory are established and the observable implication of that theory are identified, then the research can be designed in such a way as to provide the best set of comparisons given the available resources (p. 291).

The pursuit of a comparative project without an understanding and appreciation of theory will likely result in the researcher collecting a huge amount of data and having no idea what to do with it. This approach will result in the generation of largely disjointed and descriptive accounts of countries. According to Dogan and Pelassy (1990):

> Social scientists who analyse only one country may proceed step by step, without structured hypotheses, building analytical categories as they go. Comparativists have no such freedom. They cannot advance without tools. Confronted with a variety of contexts, they are obliged to rely on abstractions, to master concepts general enough to cope with the diversity of the cases under investigation (p. 3).

As Dogan and Pelassy imply, it is theory that provides the necessary tools to carry out the job of making comparisons. The task *may* be possible without them, but it is much harder to achieve and the analyses is not likely to be as insightful as that guided by theory.

Traditional comparative work has often been criticised for being atheoretical (Dogan & Pelassy, 1990; Hantrais, 2009; Øyen, 1990). This trend is evident in earlier comparative work in sport which has also been atheoretical (Henry et al., 2005). Early comparative work in sport focused on descriptive accounts of different contexts. Comparative sport scholars have increasingly started to develop theoretical frameworks for underpinning their studies. Green and Houlihan (2005), for example, utilised Sabatier and Jenkins-Smith's (1993) Advocacy Coalition Framework (ACF) to underpin their analysis of elite sport policy change within three countries. Andersen and Ronglan (2012) adapted Di Maggio and Powell's (1983) insights regarding convergence in institutional settings to analyse elite sport systems in Norway. Green (2007) and Green and Collins (2008) employed policy transfer, lesson learning and path dependency theories to explain elite sport development in the UK, Australia and Finland. Theoretical approaches such as these enable researchers to identify explanatory factors (and the interaction among factors) through applying the range of discrete factors contained within each theoretical framework to the specific focus of study.

LEVEL OF ANALYSIS – MACRO, MESO AND MICRO

In this final section, we begin to examine how the different underlying motivations for carrying out comparative research influence more fundamental methodological decisions regarding comparative design. As a result of the complexity of the social world and the need to focus comparative inquiry to identify the explanatory factors that lead to certain outcomes, comparative researchers often necessarily delimit their study to a particular level of analysis. The level of analysis can be understood as "the degree to which political units are aggregated for comparative analysis" (Landman & Carvalho, 2017, p. 306). It should be acknowledged from the outset that the level of analysis is dictated by philosophical assumptions as to what is knowable and how it can be known, which is connected to methodological choices regarding the overall focus of the study (Baistow, 2000; Dogan & Pelassy, 1990; Dowling et al., 2018; Hantrais, 2009; Jowell, 1998; Kohn, 1987; Øyen, 1990; Ragin, 2014).

In general, social scientists often refer to three levels of analysis – the macro, meso or micro level. Comparativists attempt to study these different levels of society, as well as the interactions and interconnectedness between them. The macro level refers to broad social structures, institutions and the relationship between them. Macro-level factors are deep-seated structures, social processes and trends, such as stability and change within economies, political systems or bureaucracies. Macro-level analysis is often associated with the works of traditional sociologists such as Émile Durkheim or Karl Marx, who were interested in generating 'grand theories' which explain universal social behaviour or problems. The meso level focuses on intermediate structure and processes, such as formal institutions, organisations and policy processes. It attempts to examine the middle ground and bridge the gap between the macro and micro levels. Researchers who focus on the meso level study policy processes, dominant interests, coalitions or groups, the interactions between them and the ways in which the internal and external environment dialectically relates to these issues. The micro level refers to the study of the nature of human interactions and the relationship between individuals or small groups. For example, this might include the daily interactions between coaches and athletes. The focus here is on the everyday social interaction between people.

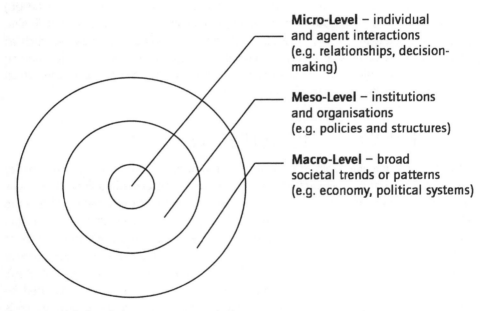

Micro-Level – individual and agent interactions (e.g. relationships, decision-making)

Meso-Level – institutions and organisations (e.g. policies and structures)

Macro-Level – broad societal trends or patterns (e.g. economy, political systems)

Figure 3.1: Level of analysis – macro, meso and micro

De Bosscher et al. (2006) discuss the application of these levels to elite sport systems and sporting success by arguing that macro-level factors within this domain include the country's population, economic welfare, geography, politics and culture. Meso-level factors include elements of the sport system that may influence the long-term performance of an athlete, such as the organisational structure of sport. Micro-level factors are individual characteristics that directly influence the athlete, such as the coach-athlete relationship and athletes' genetics.

More recent attempts to compare elite sport systems have been predicated on the assumption that macro-level factors (i.e., GDP and population size) are significant contributors to explaining the variance between elite sport success. According to De Bosscher et al.'s (2006) review of the elite sport policy/management literature, these two factors explain approximately 50% of the variance that exists between sporting nations. De Bosscher and colleagues then use this interpretation as the basis for their rationale and the need to explain the remaining 50% of variance, which they argue can be explained through the identification of structural, meso-level factors, such as facilities, scientific research and support, talent ID and development. Other researchers have highlighted the importance of different macro-level factors that have driven elite sport investment, such as globalisation, commercialisation, governmentalisation, professionalisation and politicisation (Bergsgard et al., 2007; Houlihan & Green, 2008). Green's (2005) assessment of elite sport policy change in Australia, Canada and the United Kingdom demonstrates the utility of integrating macro and meso levels of analysis. He argues that it is not possible to separate the macro and meso levels and that the inclusion of the macro level provides a more nuanced understanding of policy change.

Quite to what extent it may or may not be possible to separate the macro, meso and micro levels of analysis to make comparisons remains a point of theoretical and empirical debate within the comparative literature in general. These broader debates are also reflected within the comparative sport policy/management literature, whereby there appears to be a relatively clear divide between those who have acknowledged that nations are inextricably linked to macro-level concerns (economic, political, population, etc.) and those who deliberately choose to ignore or overlook these broader contextual factors, instead focusing on the more controllable meso level. Ragin (2014) describes the former as *comparativists*, those who choose to deliberately engage with or define macro entities, and *non-comparativists*, who treat such notions as abstractions that need not be operationalised.

Ragin's *non-comparativist* approach appears to be particularly evident in the SPLISS 1.0 and 2.0 studies by De Bosscher and colleagues (De Bosscher et al., 2006, 2015) who, while giving mention to macro-level factors, made the methodological decision to focus exclusively on the meso-level policies and process by arguing that these were the only factors in control of decision-makers. In contrast, many other comparative sport scholars (e.g., Andersen & Ronglan, 2012; Bergsgard et al., 2007; Green & Houlihan, 2005; Houlihan & Green, 2008) have rejected the notion that it is possible to fully separate policies and politics (i.e., meso level) from the broader historical, cultural and political context in which sport systems operated (i.e., macro level). The adoption of this *comparativist* (Ragin, 2014) viewpoint has led to these researchers giving explicit consideration of the broader macro-level factors in their analysis of elite sport systems.

The inherent danger of these types of debates is that they are often symptomatic of more general differences in philosophical traditions, and therefore run the risk of talking past one another (Grix, 2010). In reality, the choice of the level of analysis and the selection of the micro, meso and macro levels reflects a broader meta-philosophical debate within social research which either emphasises the role and agency of individual actors, or focuses on institutions and structures, a debate that is otherwise known as the 'agency-structure' debate (Bryman, 2015; Landman & Carvalho, 2017).

A final point of consideration concerns the extent to whether it is possible to fully separate these levels of analysis. This largely depends upon the researchers' philosophical assumptions. Nonetheless, there are two potential issues or shortcomings with choosing to separate these analytical levels. First is the twin problem of *ecological* or *individualist* fallacies which occur when a study seeks to make inferences about one level of analysis by using evidence from another (Landman & Carvalho, 2017). An ecological fallacy occurs when inferences are drawn about the individual level from aggregate-level data, and an individual fallacy occurs when data from the individual level are used to make inferences about the aggregate level (Landman & Carvalho, 2017). Landman and Carvalho (2017) identify many potential sources of these fallacies including philosophical disposition and data availability. They suggest that the best way to avoid these issues is to "minimise the chain of inference between the theoretical concepts that are specified and the measures of those concepts that are ultimately adopted in the analysis" (Landman & Carvalho, 2017, p. 52). The second potential shortcoming (or trade-off depending on one's viewpoint) is the extent to which separating analytical levels accurately reflects social reality. As intimated previously, the overall purpose of carrying out comparative inquiry is to develop theory to explain social reality. For Przeworski and Teune (1970):

> What is important for comparative inquiry is that systems with which we ordinarily deal, which as societies, nations and cultures, are organized in terms of several levels of components and that the interactions within these systems are not limited to any particular level but cut across these levels (p. 12).

Researchers looking to make meaningful comparisons must acknowledge both the existence of all levels and the interaction between them. Any attempt to focus on a specific level of analysis, whilst understandable, is nonetheless open to potential criticism as it is likely to simplify what is otherwise a more complicated reality. Przeworski and Teune's remarks here are also congruent with Jowell's (1998) recommendation that "cross-national [research] should pay as much attention to the choice and compilation of aggregate-level contextual variables as they do individual-level dependent and independent variables" (p. 174). In practice, then, any attempt to separate these levels – whilst practically/methodologically convenient, does not necessarily reflect social reality.

CHAPTER SUMMARY

In summary, this chapter has addressed fundamental questions regarding why we seek to make comparisons. To this end, it has outlined the various motivations which underpin comparative inquiry by drawing upon and elaborating on some general and sport-specific typologies that have attempted to categorise the different underlying reasons/motivations for carrying out comparative research. In doing so, the chapter has also discussed the role of theory and how this underpins comparative inquiry, as well as how these varying underlying approaches lead to the adoption of different methodological approaches. The chapter ended with a consideration of how different motivations and rationales inform more specific methodological choices, such as the unit of analysis selected. The next part of the book (part 2) considers the methodological decisions and trade-offs faced by those that seek to make comparisons.

CASE STUDY 3: A TYPOLOGY OF APPROACHES TO COMPARATIVE SPORT POLICY ANALYSIS (HENRY ET AL., 2005)

When engaging with any research it is necessary for the critical mind to remain cognisant of the ontological and epistemological assumptions that guide the research process. Differing philosophical perspectives provide a different view of reality, and, therefore competing interpretations of how the social world can be known (Blaikie, 1993). For positivists, reality consists of what is available to the senses (Bryman, 2015). In other words, positivists recognise reality through facts and figures that can be observed, measured and understood (Sparkes, 1992). For positivists, reality and knowledge are free from the values attributed to them by individuals (Bryman, 2015). In contrast, interpretivism is humanistic; knowledge is a human construction acquired through individual interpretations of social reality (Blaikie, 1993; Sparkes, 1992). Thus, interpretivism emphasises individual experience, belief and understanding, and consequently, 'social reality is the product of processes by which social actors together negotiate the meaning for actions and situations' (Blaikie, 1993, p. 96). Importantly, such interpretations are not fixed, but open to constant construction and refinement. Recognising and understanding the differences in these philosophical positions is necessary as it provides insight into the value, limitations and differences of each position, and helps to avoid the philosophical trap. This trap emerges when researchers critique one another's work without taking into account the philosophical position that undergirds the research. As a result, researchers continue to argue past each other

(Grix, 2010) as they fail to recognise the purpose, possibilities and limitations of the research as directed by the philosophical perspective.

When contemplating ontological considerations in the comparative context, it is helpful to reflect upon the underlying motivations that guide the work as they reveal much about the reality that the researcher seeks to explore. For some (such as Digel, 2002), comparative work is driven by a desire to gain a deeper sense of a particular nation or recognising similarities and differences with other countries. Such work can be said to align more clearly with the interpretivist or post-positivist perspective, as it seeks to interpret the meaning of policy and practice as represented by policy agents (or secondarily through policy-based documentation). For others (such as De Bosscher, 2006), it is about identifying causal factors and using discrete quantitative methods to demonstrate how such factors contribute to international success. Research of this type more clearly aligns with the positivist perspective insofar as it seeks to measure numerical data, despite this numerical data being value-laden based upon the perspective of the researcher, athlete, coach or performance director responding to the survey. Thus, while the research ideologically aligns with a particular philosophy, it is methodologically misaligned as the instrumentation fails to achieve the ideals of the philosophy underpinning it.

Henry et al. (2005) have advanced the debate on the different types of comparative research in sport through their four-fold typology of comparative sports policy studies. This typology helps to identity and group different types of comparative sport research, for example:

Type 1 'Seeking Similarities': a nomothetic approach to seeking law-like genera-lisations. Gratton et al.'s (2011) study of comparisons in sports participation across European countries is an example of type 1. This project sought to identify explanations for different patterns of participation across European countries.

Type 2 'Describing Difference': an ideographic approach that seeks to capture the specificity of policy systems. Houlihan's (1997) use of Down's sequential model of the policy process helps to guide his study of five countries to identify and describe the key differences (and similarities) in how different nations go about developing policy to address issues concerning physical education in schools and drugs in sport.

Type 3 'Theorizing the Transnational': this approach goes beyond national borders to examine a combination of local and global factors. Houlihan and

Green's (2008) examination of elite sport systems, structures and policies in nine countries addresses transnational concerns, particularly the significance of mechanisms for convergence and the processes of learning to advance elite sport development internationally.

Type 4 'Defining Discourse': this approach focuses on how discourse defines policy problems. For example, Piggin et al.'s (2009) analysis of sport policy in New Zealand emphasises an approach whereby discourse analysis was used to demonstrate inherent contradictions between the rhetoric of New Zealand's sport policy and the reality of the policy system as revealed in the policy truths constructed through a variety of media (Piggin et al., 2008, p. 478).

We argue that Henry et al.'s (2005) typology is instructive for future comparative research within sport, as it highlights the dominant approaches to comparative research in sport and explicitly addresses the kinds of questions asked, the methods used and the philosophical assumptions made in each of the four types of research. If researchers were to explicitly address such issues in future work, we could develop a range of insightful research, with clear attention to the purpose, value and limitations, thereby minimising the problem of the philosophical trap and enhancing clarity of thought and clarity of ambition (Henry et al., 2008).

PART II

HOW TO COMPARE SPORTING NATIONS — METHODS, PROTOCOL AND PRACTICE

CHAPTER 4

Selecting Countries (Sampling)

Chapter objectives

- To explore the assumptions of adopting the nation state as a unit of analysis for social inquiry;
- To distinguish the sample strategies available to comparative researchers when selecting countries for comparisons;
- To discuss the potential limitations, challenges and practical implications of sampling strategies.

The selection of cases (or sample) involves deciding which particular social unit to compare and how many units to compare. In relation to the former, most comparative research takes as its initial point of departure the nation state. As will be gathered by the reader, there are many good reasons for adopting the nation state as the analytical level of choice, however, this decision may not be as straightforward as it may initially seem. This chapter explores this assumption and considers the potential implications of either utilising or not utilising the nation state for those seeking to make comparisons in sport. Following this, comparative researchers need to decide how they will go about selecting countries for comparison. This is also not an easy task as there are fundamental differences and methodological trade-offs that require consideration. In general, the selection strategy is either a 'Most Similar System Design' (MSSD), which involves the selection of countries that are as similar as possible, or a 'Most Different System Design' (MDSD), whereby countries are selected based on being as different as possible. As will become apparent, these approaches have considerable implications for the rationale and practical decisions relating to which countries are included or excluded and why. These approaches and their assumptions, challenges and limitations are discussed below.

With regard to how many units to compare, far from being yet another arbitrary methodological decision, the choice and selection of cases depends on a range of factors. These include the philosophical underpinning of the research, the overall intention and purpose of the investigation, the research question posed, the general methodological approach adopted and the practicalities associated with accessing data. These approaches can generally be categorised into those which include many cases in their sample (large-N) and those with a few (small-N). Both of these approaches involve methodological trade-offs and both sampling strategies must be carried out with caution as they can be subject to many pitfalls, such as the *'too many variables, not enough cases'* dilemma and the *'problem of contingency'* (Ebbinghaus, 2005; Landman & Carvalho, 2017; Lijphart, 1971).

This chapter begins by exploring the appropriateness of the nation state, the analytical level of choice and the challenges of this commonly held assumption that permeates much of the comparative tradition. Although it is acknowledged that there is a qualitative distinction between the term country and the nation state – with the former often defined based on being a geo-political boundary and the latter more accurately a reflection of some socio-cultural divide – for the sake of the present discussion these units are assumed to be synonymous throughout. Next, both large-N and small-N sampling approaches are discussed along with their respective challenges and limitations. Although comparative inquiry has traditionally been dominated by large-N studies, it is argued that both these approaches have the potential to contribute to our understanding of sport. This is preceeded by an in-depth discussion of the process for deciding which cases should be selected, which usually occurs through either the adoption of an MSSD or MDSD sampling approach. Each of these approaches and their implications for methodological design and limitations of knowledge claims are then discussed. The final section considers how it may be possible to reconcile these sampling strategies to produce more robust sampling approaches for comparison.

THE NATION STATE – APPROPRIATE UNIT OF ANALYSIS?

The nation state is a common choice of unit of analysis for comparative inquiry as it is relatively stable, enduring and homogeneous (Dogan & Pelassy, 1990; Hantrais, 2009; Jowell, 1998; Landman & Carvalho, 2017; Øyen, 1990; Przeworski & Teune, 1970; Teune, 1990). The rationale for why comparative researchers select nations states is understandable as:

> ...the world is divided according to these administrative units (countries), and since much of the infrastructure available for comparative research is tied to the territories enclosed by national boundaries, it becomes seductively convincing to use such units in comparative studies (Øyen, 1990, p. 2).

The nation state is such a commonly held assumption in comparative research that "one can hardly escape from using the nation level" (Hofstede, 1998, p. 17). Despite its inescapability, the selection of the nation state for comparative analysis is a methodological decision and represents "but one type of comparison of human systems" (Teune, 1990, p. 38). Therefore, it is necessary, at minimum, to recognise the limitations of the approach and the normative value attached to it. To begin to appreciate the limitations of choosing countries as the appropriate unit of analysis, consider the following thought exercise:

Let us imagine a nation, perhaps on a remote island that has never been explored by 'outsiders'. If you were to visit this new country, what would you choose to see? Who would you select to describe this 'newfound' nation? How would you establish the nature and extent of the social structures that exist within the country? What would you choose to record? What questions would you ask or what measurements would you decide to take? What would you decide to focus on and why to explain what you saw to those back at home? Assuming that you know nothing about the country in question, how would you explore the underlying mechanisms within that society beyond observation? How would you know that what you asked in one part of the country is the same in another? In other words, would your observations hold for the entire country?

The answers to these questions are not easy to answer and the remote island thought exercise serves to highlight the extent of the challenge and difficulties that lie ahead of those seeking to make comparisons through the adoption of the nation state lens.

Within sport, the assumption is that nation states are the most appropriate unit of analysis to make comparisons on the basis that they are commonly understood and that many international sporting events use national boundaries as the dominant criteria to structure international competitions. The International Olympic Committee (IOC), for example, currently recognises a total of 206 nations or member countries. There are, however, conceptual and practical issues with selecting the nation state to make comparisons in sport, including defining and changing geo-political boundaries and the heterogeneity that exists within a nation. In regards to the former, geo-political boundaries can be subject to considerable change. Examples include the dissolution of the Soviet Union and the former Yugoslavia which led to a debate concerning international recognition of the successor states or the peculiarity of the United Kingdom which is permitted to enter four countries (i.e., the 'home nations' which, taken together, constitute what is generally recognised as the nation state) under the single banner of "Team GB". Secondly, some national boundaries are subject to intense negotiation and renegotiation that may occur by conflict (e.g., South Sudan and the Republic of Sudan). Such problems do not consider other extremes such as addressing the issue of athletes that are either disassociated through their refugee status (reflected in the formation of a Refugee team), claim no nationality at all (neutral athletes) or have their origins from countries that are not formally recognised by the International Olympic Committee.

Another problem with the nation state as a unit of analysis is that of heterogeneity. Even in cases where the nation state is perceived to be relatively stable there can be huge variation within and amongst the population. Canada, for example, has longstanding issues of unity, namely the sovereignty and separation of the province of Quebec. The United States of America is technically a confederation of nation states and self-governing territories with considerable socio-cultural differences between them. Similarly, the United Kingdom's exit from the European Union, and the continued political debate regarding the potential future devolution of its home nations, are all contemporary examples of differences within nations and changing geo-political boundaries. The above examples also highlight much broader issues of national heterogeneity, in that even the most stable and homogenous nation states have fundamentally different cultural, ethnic and social boundaries within them. There can be as much variation between regions within a nation, as between separate nations. It is perhaps for this reason that Dogan and Pelassy (1990, p. 18) identified "eight Spains,...four Finlands,...three Belgiums, four Italys, and five or six Frances".

Furthermore, this *within-country* variation can be different depending on the context or issue. As Øyen (1990, p. 49) points out, "a country may be a country for certain kinds of things – sports, for example – but not for others". This raises more fundamental issues about whether there is less variation within countries than there is across them. Dogan and Pelassy (1990) suggest that there may be equal, if not greater, value in comparing municipalities, states, regions, provinces and/or territories, which are arguably more stable and less heterogeneous domains than that of the precarious, malleable and constantly changing nation state. Currently, there are surprisingly few studies within sport in general, and the sport policy/management domain in particular, that compare intra-variation within countries. Examples of potential comparative studies that could be conducted include comparing sport systems across provinces/territories/states within federated systems such as Canada, Australia and the United States or intra-country comparisons of the home nations within the UK (England, Northern Ireland, Scotland and Wales). These comparisons could be particularly fruitful given the underlying similarity of each of the cases, which would enable the researcher to identify the variables or factors that explain the differences observed.

In summary, despite the commonly held assumption and the obvious appeal of selecting nation states as the basis for comparisons, the limitations of this approach should be acknowledged. In doing so, it may be possible to build in strategies to mitigate against some of these limitations, including utilising researchers from within the local context or considering whether it is possible to compare *within* rather than across nations. In assuming that the nation state is selected by comparative researchers to conduct their analysis, it is necessary to consider the process for selecting countries for comparison. An overview of this process follows the next subsection which explores the main sampling strategies that can be used to make comparisons: comparing many (or large-N), comparing few (small-N) or single-country studies.

LARGE-N/SMALL-N APPROACHES TO COMPARISON

In addition to deciding whether the nation state is an appropriate unit for analysis, the comparative researcher needs to make another important methodological decision regarding how many countries to include for comparison (Ebbinghaus, 2005; Hantrais, 2009; Jowell, 1998; Landman & Carvalho, 2017; Ragin, 2006, 2014). It is a commonplace question for anyone seeking to conduct any type of research – how many participants do I need for my study? The same issues apply to cross-national research. Much in the same way as any research project, the short answer to the question of how many participants do I need, is that it depends. The longer answer is that there is a methodological trade-off to be made between selecting few participants (or countries) in an efficient and resource-effective manner, but not too few participants/countries which would run the risk of under-representation and lack of generalisability. Equally, too many participants/countries may generate vast data sets that require extensive data reduction strategies, which is resource-intensive and runs the potential risk of data overload or improper use.

In an attempt to categorise these methodological tendencies with regards to selecting countries, Landman and Carvalho (2017) identified three general strategies: comparing many countries, comparing few countries and conducting single-country studies. The decision to adopt either approach (i.e., 'many' countries or 'few' countries) is largely dependent upon several factors including the underlying philosophical assumptions, the motivations for carrying out the study, the research question posited and the methods preferred by the comparative researcher (Landman & Carvalho, 2017). Both these approaches have relative strengths and weaknesses and are equally susceptible to issues of non-sample equivalence (Ebbinghaus, 2005) discussed below.

According to Landman and Carvalho (2017), studies which include many countries lead to large-scale, variable-oriented comparisons, often through statistical inferences by controlling for other variables. Comparing fewer countries, on the other hand, involves a focused comparison of select cases in a more intensive manner, attempting to understand the nuance of each case that may take into account the macro, meso and micro factors. It is also possible to use a single country with many observations for comparisons (Landman & Carvalho, 2017). Single cases such as these (often outlier or extreme cases) are particularly useful for comparative research as they produce rich, contextual description and help generate new theory (Eisenhardt, 1989). Examples of detailed descriptive accounts of elite sport systems include Bergsgard and Norberg (2010), who attempt to identify a common elite sport model across Scandinavian countries, and Darko and Mackintosh (2015) who examine the challenges and constraints of implementing sport policy in the small states of Antigua and Barbuda, as well as expose the contestations that occur between elite sport and participation agendas. These studies have provided important groundwork for the development of social theory and the institutionalisation and prioritisation of elite sport in western nations and small-states respectively.

Many other comparativists prefer the distinction between large-N (i.e., many countries) and small-N studies (i.e., few/single countries), with the former focusing on general dimensions and the relationships between variables at a higher level of abstraction, and the latter emphasising an intensive contextual analysis of a select few cases (countries) at a low to medium level of abstraction. Table 4.1 provides an overview of large-N and small-N sampling approaches.

Table 4.1: Overview of large-N and small-N sampling approaches

	Large-N	Small-N
Number of cases	>20	5-19
Sample selection	Random/stratified	Purposeful
Emphasis	Extensive	Intensive
Theory	Theory building and testing	Theory building
Approach	Variable focused	Case based
Analysis	Quantitative	Qualitative
Strengths	Internal validity	External validation
Weaknesses	• Finding cases • Non-random sample • Problem of contingency	• Finding cases • Problem of contingency

As large-N studies focus on the relationship between variables, they tend to involve an extensive examination of social phenomena, following the typical rules of statistical inference by controlling for any confounding factors and randomising country selection in an attempt to avoid selection bias, although as we will discuss, this is not always possible. In contrast, small-N studies emphasise an intensive examination of a select number of countries whereby countries are selected purposefully to make meaningful comparisons. It is for these reasons that large-N type studies are associated with the variable-oriented approaches, which often employ quantitative techniques and small-N with the case-oriented and qualitative approaches.

There is no agreed-upon number of cases that defines either a large-N or small-N study, however, the general consensus within the comparative literature is that large-N refers to 20 countries or greater (Ebbinghaus, 2005; Hantrais, 2009; Landman & Carvalho, 2017). By this definition (i.e., large-N >20), most of the comparative research within the sport policy/ management domain can be described as small-N studies ranging from 2-15 nations. The closest to a large-N study would be De Bosscher et al.'s (2015) SPLISS 2.0 study.

Large-N studies are particularly suitable for empirically testing theory against pre-determined hypotheses. A notable strength of the large-N approach is that it can control (or at least partially control) for extraneous variables that might explain the outcome observed. It is for this reason that many consider this to be the 'gold standard' approach to making comparisons (Lijphart, 1971). This is because large-N approaches have strong internal validity, as additional controls can be added to isolate causal effects. In contrast, small-N studies that involve a case-study approach are applied in 'real-life' rather than artificial settings, and are therefore seen to have stronger external validity and can be generalised beyond the specific context in question.

Both large-N and small-N sampling approaches face difficulties in being able to find a suitable number of countries to include in the sample. This is a common criticism of the comparative approach (Lijphart, 1971), particularly where a number of countries are needed in order to facilitate an appropriate comparison based upon the number of potentially relevant variables sought (Ebbinghaus, 2005). This is often referred to as the 'too many variables and not enough cases' problem (Dogan & Pelassy, 1990; Ebbinghaus, 2005; Landman & Carvalho, 2017; Lijphart, 1971). This problem occurs when there are too many variables or explanatory factors that can explain the observed outcome than there are number of countries sampled in the study. The outcome of this is an indeterminant study design, because it is not possible to identify and distinguish explanatory factors that share some form of relationship outcomes. Lijphart (1971) identifies four potential solutions to the 'too many variables small-N' problem including increasing the number of cases (where possible), combining variables to have fewer variables, focusing on comparative cases and only focusing on key variables.

Some researchers within the comparative sport domain have adopted solutions to avoid the too many variables, small-N predicament. De Bosscher and colleagues (De Bosscher et al., 2009, 2015), for example, reduced their number of critical success factors (variables) from 105 to 96 between SPLISS 1.0 and SPLISS 2.0 studies. Also, they recruited an international team of researchers, sought government funding in each locale and developed complex and comprehensive operational protocols to collect data across multiple countries. De Bosscher et al.'s (2015) SPLISS 2.0 study involved 58 researchers and 22 policy-makers from 15 nations. Countries were invited to participate via email and conference presentations to a wide network of sport policy scholars and sport administrators. Invitations to participate in the project were made based on their willingness and ability to independently co-ordinate and collect the necessary data. The practical and logistical realities of this approach, however, meant that the principal researcher was required to identify a researcher (or a research team) within each country with the interest and capacity to engage in the comparative research process. This could potentially result in co-investigators with a self-selection bias.

Yet another weakness of both large-N and small-N approaches is the assumption that large-N studies are randomised and that small-N studies are purposefully selected from a sample population. Large-N studies assume homogeneity and that the more nations included the better, but continually adding more countries becomes increasingly problematic and data availability across an entire sample population is rare. Quite often large-N approaches involve the selection of countries from using the 'best available' data, which might be compiled by third-party organisations, such as the European Commission or the International Olympic Committee. Not only do these data sets have considerable limitations in their own right (see chapter 5 on equivalence), but they are based upon a particular sub-set of countries rather than the entire sample population. Ebbinghaus (2005) refers to this limitation as the *'problem of contingency'*, as it involves the pre-selection of cases based upon historical and political processes. Ebbinghaus (2005) argues that all comparative research including large-N or small-N approaches is subject to the problem of contingency, but that large-N studies are particularly susceptible due to the assumption of randomisation. Thus, large-N studies may proffer the 'illusion of sampling' insofar as they suggest that they have a random sample, but in reality, they have a pseudo-randomised or stratified sample based on pre-selected nations (Ebbinghaus, 2005).

Another potential limitation linked to the problem of contingency is *selection bias* (Ebbinghaus, 2005; Geddes, 1990; Hug, 2003; Landman & Carvalho, 2017). This form of bias involves the intentional or unintentional inclusion of cases that support the theory being tested. This can also include more subtle forms of selection bias such as choice of a country based on the dependent variable, the selection of certain sources of information and the ignoring of others, and an over-emphasis on particular outcomes (Landman & Carvalho, 2017). As indicated, the problem of selection bias can occur entirely unintentionally rather than through a deliberate act of manipulation. Both scenarios – whether intentional or unintentional – can lead to an overestimation of the explanatory factors, resulting in inaccurate or even indeterminant findings. Potential strategies for mitigating against the problem of contingency and selection bias include: a clear and explicit articulation of methods in general and the sampling and procedures specifically, recognising the limitations of the sample selected (which is more likely to be stratified rather than random) and a recognition of the researcher-bias within the research process.

LARGE-N/SMALL-N – THE METHODOLOGICAL TRADE-OFF

Whilst the distinctions between many, few or singular and large-N versus small-N approaches to sample selection are apparent within all comparative research traditions, it is perhaps more appropriate to recognise that these general strategies are more accurately a continuum – from studies of N=1 at one end to studies which include the entire sample population at the other. The more countries that are included, the greater the need for the higher-order abstraction of concepts to be able to make meaningful comparisons. Equally, the lower the number of countries, the lower the level of abstraction. Landman and Carvalho (2017) describe the issue of selecting countries more generally as a methodological trade-off between the level of abstraction and the scope of countries under examination (see Figure 4.1).

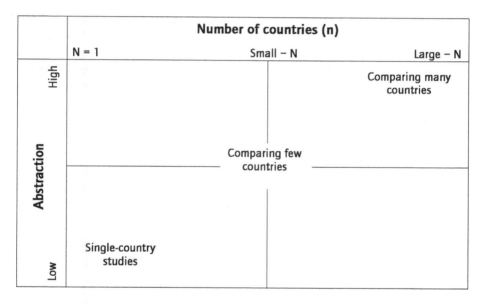

Figure 4.1: Landman and Carvalho's scope-abstraction *methodological trade-off*
Adapted from: Landman and Carvalho (2017)

The implication of these methodological trade-offs is large-N studies require the use of more abstract concepts to make comparisons, whereas small-N studies can be more specific in their analytical approach.

To summarise the discussion so far, many comparative researchers adopt the nation state as their unit of analysis for comparisons. This is both understandable and problematic. Assuming that countries are selected as the unit for comparison, the researcher must then decide whether to include many countries and a large-N sample or few countries and a small-N sample. Both of these approaches have fundamentally different focuses, approaches, and strengths and weaknesses. A final methodological question beyond whether to include many or few countries is, How exactly do comparative researchers decide which countries to include and why? What are the inclusion criteria by which countries should be selected? This range of issues should be fully considered prior to the finalisation of the methodological design. The next section gives attention to sampling and questions about which countries to select and why.

MOST SIMILAR SYSTEM DESIGNS/MOST DIFFERENT SYSTEM DESIGNS

Two general approaches can be used to select countries to make comparisons: Most Similar System Designs (MSSD) and Most Different System Designs (MDSD). Table 4.2 provides an overview of both these strategies. To understand the differences between these approaches, it is worth drawing upon a simplified example of scenarios. Imagine that a family goes out to a restaurant for a meal. After they arrive home from the meal, all but one of them feels unwell. Assuming all other factors are controlled for (*ceteris paribus*), then it is possible to determine which food caused the illness.

MSSD – Method of difference

	Prawns	Steak	Pasta	Salad	Feels unwell?
Mum	Yes	Yes	Yes	Yes	Yes
Dad	Yes	Yes	Yes	Yes	Yes
Daughter	Yes	Yes	Yes	Yes	Yes
Son	No	Yes	Yes	Yes	No

Now imagine a different scenario in which all of them felt unwell and they all had a variety of different options on the menu.

MDSD – Method of agreement

	Prawns	Steak	Pasta	Salad	Feels unwell?
Mum	No	Yes	Yes	Yes	Yes
Dad	Yes	Yes	No	Yes	Yes
Daughter	Yes	Yes	Yes	No	Yes
Son	Yes	Yes	Yes	Yes	Yes

In this case, it is possible to identify which factor was common across all family members. If everyone had the steak, then we can infer that it was the steak that caused everyone to be unwell.

The first scenario is a simplified version of the MSSD approach in that all factors or variables (meals) are the same across all cases (family members), with the exception of the one key factor (prawns). The MSSD approach is primarily based upon John Stuart Mills's (1843) *method of difference* (see box below) which states that "if an instance in which the phenomenon under investigation occurs, and an instance in which it does not occur, have every circumstance save one in common, that one occurring only in the former; the circumstance in which alone the two instances differ, is the effect, or cause, or a necessary part of the cause, of the phenomenon" (p. 455). In applying this logic of inference, those utilising the MSSD approach select cases (nations) that have as many similar features as possible with exception of the key factor or the variable that the researcher seeks to explore (see the left side of Table 4.2). The assumption is that if a researcher can control as many confounding extraneous variables as possible, then a researcher is more likely to be able to isolate which factors might be causing a particular outcome.

In discussing the MSSD approach, Przeworski and Teune (1970) state that "most comparative studies take as their point of departure the known differences among social systems and examine the impact of these differences on some other social phenomena observed within these systems" (p. 31). They go on to argue that "within this strategy [MSSD], differences among systems are taken into account as they are encountered in the process of explaining social phenomena observed within these systems" (*ibid*).

*Mills, J. (1842). A Systemic of Logic: Ratiocinative and Inductive: London: Parker

In his foundational works, philosopher Mills outlined five methods of inductive logic to identify causal connections: direct method of agreement, method of difference, joint method of agreement and difference; method of residue and method of concomitant variations. Ironically, although Mills argued that it was not appropriate to apply his inductive logic to the social sciences (Lijphart, 1971, p. 65), his work has been particularly influential within the comparative sociology domain.

In their seminal works, Przeworski and Teune outlined an alternative approach to the MSSD, which they call the 'Most Different System Design' (MDSD). This approach is illustrated in the second restaurant scenario whereby through a process of elimination it is possible to establish that everyone felt unwell because of the steak. The MDSD, in contrast, is based upon Mill's (1843) *method of agreement,* which states that, *"if two or more instances of the phenomenon under investigation have only one circumstance in common, the circumstance in which alone all the instances agree, is the cause (or effect) of the given phenomenon"* (p. 454). Unlike the MSSD approach, the MDSD deliberately selects cases (nations) that have different features, thereby controlling for these potentially confounding variables to identify the key factor that is common across all cases (see right side of Table 4.2).

Table 4.2: Most Similar System Design (MSSD) and Most Different System Designs (MDSD)

	Most Similar System Design (MSSD)			Most Different System Design (MDSD)		
Variables	Country A	Country B	Country C	Country A	Country B	Country C
I^1	a	a	a	a	d	g
I^2	b	b	b	b	e	h
I^3	c	c	c	c	f	i
Key factor	x	x	not x	x	x	x

Adapted from: Anckar (2008); Carvalho and Landman (2017); Przeworski and Teune (1970)

In comparing sporting nations, researchers that employ a MSSD are likely to select nations based on their having similar systemic features such as political and welfare systems, socio-demographics, historical background, etc. This approach requires researchers to identify 'like-for-like' countries to make meaningful comparisons. For this reason, it is common for researchers that utilise a MSSD strategy to adopt 'area-based studies' that involve the selection of nations that share many similar features, such as their geographical proximity (e.g., Scandinavia) or cultural identity (e.g., Latin America). As an example from the elite sport policy/management literature, Andersen and Ronglan (2012) adopted a MSSD approach to their analysis of elite sport development by selecting like-for-like countries (Norway, Denmark, Sweden and Finland) all within the Nordic region. The authors' assumption is that many factors (geographic size, political ideology and systems, welfare state arrangements, etc.) can be controlled for and therefore it is possible to identify more precisely the explanatory factors, which in this case were the pressures leading to increasing similarity of emphasis on elite sport success within these nations. The assumption made by those who adopt a MSSD is that, "systems as similar as possible with respect to as many features as possible constitute the optimal samples for comparative inquiry" (Przeworski & Teune, 1970, p. 32).

As a consequence of this approach, those who adopt a MSSD approach tend to find countries that are as similar as possible to keep as many confounding factors constant, thereby making it easier to identify any explanatory factors. The commonly held assumption by those who adopt a MSSD approach is that the common system features are 'controlled for' and are irrelevant and any differences observed can be attributed to explanatory variables. The adoption of the MSSD, and the selection of similar countries, presume that if some important differences can be found, then the number of explanatory variables that could explain them would be so few that it is possible to identify the likely explanatory factors (Przeworski & Teune, 1970).

In practice, there remains the possibility of other explanatory factors that have not been considered, or perhaps have been considered, but are not entirely controlled for. Thus, the inherent risk of adopting this approach is an overdetermination of the explanatory variable (Przeworski & Teune, 1970), which could also be explained by some yet unidentified or controlled for variable. As a result, researchers adopting a MSSD approach often cannot say definitively what the explanatory factors are, and therefore tend to be cautious about generalising their findings beyond the specific cases. There is the additional consideration that finding enough similar countries is often very difficult, if not impractical, and as a consequence, it may not be possible to control for all potential confounding variables. In considering the practical application of this approach, what are the chances of finding enough similar countries that are alike on many variables, except the one explanatory variable? The answer is quite unlikely. A useful distinction is provided by Anckar (2008, p. 390), who distinguishes between the 'strict' application of the MSSD, whereby countries are selected based on having many similar specified variables and different only with respect to the independent variable and a 'looser' application of this logic, whereby the sample is derived from similar or like-for-like nations. Many studies within the elite sport policy domain have chosen the latter, primarily due to the practical impossibilities of finding countries that are so similar save the independent variable in question.

In contrast, researchers who adopt a MDSD are likely to select sporting nations who share the same outcome but have different system features. The focus here is on selecting countries that are as different as possible, with an emphasis on the dependent rather than independent variables. The selection of different countries enables a researcher "to identify those independent variables, observed within systems, that do not violate the assumption of the homogeneity of the total population" (Przeworski & Teune, 1970, p. 35). The assumption made by those who adopt the MDSD approach is that all dependent variables do not change and are held constant, and that the sample from which samples are drawn are homogenous. A key distinguishing feature between the MDSD and the MSSD approach is that the former emphasises system factors and the latter often lower sub-system level factors (Przeworski & Teune, 1970). The major limitation of the MDSD is that it can only be employed where the dependent variables investigated are at the lower/sub-system level (Anckar, 2008; Przeworski & Teune, 1970). This often makes the deployment of the MDSD approach nonapplicable for most comparative research. This shortcoming is reflected within the elite sport policy/management literature, with very few attempts to apply this logic to compare elite sport systems. Perhaps the closest example to this approach in a sport context is Digel (2002, 2005) who attempted to determine why the top ten sporting nations were more successful than others in track and field athletics. The explanatory outcome (dependent variable) in this case is consistent medal success at the Olympic Games and World Championships. Digel's analysis identified a number of societal, organisational and societal-organisational relationship factors that influence high performance success – many of which were sub-system rather than system-level factors.

CHOOSING BETWEEN MSSD/MDSD APPROACHES

How, then, does a researcher decide between adopting a MSSD or a MDSD research strategy? Anckar (2008) provides a useful response to this question by identifying how and when each of these designs should be employed by comparative researchers. He argues that the choice of whether to select an MSSD or MDSD is contingent on whether the study is focused on systemic or sub-systemic levels, the deductive or inductive research strategy employed, and if the dependent variable is either constant or varied. Anckar (2008) describes all outcomes of these distinctions leading to eight potential comparative research designs that can be employed. These, in turn, lead to either a MSSD or a MDSD approach. See Anckar (2008, p. 394) for an elaboration of these study designs.

In reality, the practical application of these designs is never quite as clear-cut as the MSSD/MDSD distinctions suggest and the design is often determined by practical limitations and what the researcher is ultimately seeking to explain. For example, in attempting to apply the MSSD, it is very difficult (if not impossible) to identify another sample (nation) that shares all features but the one dependent variable which you seek to explain. The challenge for those attempting to adopt a MSSD, therefore, is being able to find enough cases that share many similar features to examine the key factors or variables. This problem is often referred to as the *"too many variables, small cases"* problem (Ebbinghaus, 2005; Landman & Carvalho, 2017) and is a common criticism of case-oriented comparative research. It is important to note that this problem is not unique to the MSSD approach and can also be an issue for those adopting MDSD approaches, especially when the number of variables is increased resulting in fewer countries that can be selected for comparison. The perennial problem of "too many variables, small cases" for MSSD approaches is perhaps why even Mills himself argued that it was not appropriate to apply his methods to the social sciences (Mills, 1872 cited in Lijphart,

1971, p. 65) and to do so "was completely out of the question". Furthermore, he argued that any attempt to do so would be a "gross misconception of the mode of investigation proper to political phenomena". Despite these rather damming remarks, Mills' work on inductive logic has been particularly influential within the comparative sociology domain. In choosing between these strategies, it is evident from the above discussion that both approaches have their associated strengths and weaknesses and involve a different logic of inquiry. With that said, "the difference between the two strategies should not be over-emphasised. Both strategies can result in the confirmation of theoretical statements and both can combine intrasystemic and intersystemic levels of analysis" (Przeworski & Teune, 1970, p. 35).

MOVING BEYOND THE MSSD/MDSD DISTINCTION

In recent years there have been attempts to overcome some of the issues and associated weaknesses of both the MSSD and MDSD approaches. Some studies within mainstream comparative politics and sociology have attempted to combine both the MSSD and MDSD approaches (e.g., De Meur & Berg-Schlosser, 1994). Others have attempted to overcome some of these issues by proposing alternative approaches. Ragin and colleagues (Ragin, 1987, 2006; Rihoux, 2006; Rihoux & Ragin, 2012), for example, developed what they described as the configurational approach and the qualitative case analysis (QCA)/ fuzzy set analysis. QCA/fuzzy set analysis combines MSSD and MDSD approaches and variable-oriented logic with a case-study approach which they argue provides a more holistic understanding of similarities and differences amongst countries. To date, none of these approaches have been adopted or applied within the sporting context, although they clearly have the potential to provide a deeper understanding of similarities and differences, both within and across sporting nations.

CHAPTER SUMMARY

In summary, this chapter has addressed a range of issues that require attention when sampling and selecting units for the basis of comparative analysis. More specifically, it has highlighted the range of assumptions that are typically associated with adopting the nation state as the unit of analysis for comparative analysis. Given that the nation state tends to be the most common unit of analysis, the chapter also provides a number of strategies that comparative researchers can use to minimise limitations. The choices between the MSSD and MDSD approaches to sampling and the potential of moving beyond such a distinction to provide a more complete analysis of the similarities and differences across countries.

CASE STUDY 4: CASE SELECTION AND THE MSSD APPROACH IN EXAMINING NORDIC ELITE SPORT POLICY (ANDERSEN & RONGLAN, 2012)

Andersen and Ronglan's study of Nordic elite sport sought to identify the similarities and differences in factors that influence elite sport in four Nordic countries in the post-Second World War era. The study is instructive to this case insofar as the methodological design emphasised an MSSD selection strategy in order to achieve the goals of the study. Four specific countries were included in the study (Denmark, Finland, Norway and Sweden) with the inclusion criteria emphasising the most similar systems, predicated on similarities in population, geographical region, welfare state arrangements, comparable social, economic and political systems, together with similar characteristics in the dominant model of sport emphasising a voluntary based sport movement with a commitment to sport for all and the instrumental value of sport participation.

The overarching purpose of the study, and the specific motivations underpinning the MSSD selection strategy, were to provide a more nuanced insight into the realities of the organisation and development of elite sport in the Nordic region. Here, the authors underline that while, as expected, there are some commonalities, it is the differences in how the four countries have developed elite sport policy and practice that are particularly striking. The MSSD strategy and the inclusion criteria used in this study were pursued to demonstrate how dominant ideas about the convergence of elite sport policy across national borders need to be synthesised with greater consideration of divergence at the national level. Similarly, the MSSD design and inclusion criteria enabled the authors to address commonly held assumptions about the development of sport in the Nordic region, and provide more precise and, in some cases, counter-intuitive insights into how each of the four Nordic countries has organised elite sport. At an empirical level, the MSSD selection strategy was supported by drawing evidence and data from a number of sources, including archival materials, policy documents, statistics and results of elite sport competitions, supplemented by interviews with leaders from National Olympic Committees, national federations of sport and national elite sport organisations in all four countries.

The results of the analysis showed that Denmark, Sweden and Finland have all historically performed much better than Norway in the summer Olympic Games. In contrast, Finland, Sweden and Norway have stronger traditions in the winter Olympic Games. The authors present results from the 1952 to 2008 games in order to facilitate a discussion of the differing trends in performance outcomes and how these outcomes, to differing degrees, have influenced policy responses to elite sport across the region. From this starting point, the authors highlight how Norway and Finland's hosting of the Summer and Winter Games in 1952, the various welfare state strategies of the four countries, and the responsibilities of domestic sport federations and NOCs, (which reflected a broad trend towards the professionalisation and rationalisation of elite sport) were the common characteristics that influenced the development of elite sport across Denmark, Finland, Norway and Sweden in the era from the 1960s to the 1990s. Alongside these commonalities, the authors stress the importance of understanding the increased divergence in timing, political processes and the nature of changes across the four countries. The analysis continues by discussing how setbacks in international sport competitions prompted a number of initiatives to strengthen elite sport in Denmark and Norway in the 1970s and 1980s. However, while they were more successful than their neighbours, the fluctuations in success in international sport in Sweden and Finland were not viewed as systemic problems and thus did not result in major changes in how elite sport was developed during the 1970s and 1980s. Similar trends appear to have continued during the period from 1990 to 2010. In short, Denmark and Norway have continued to consolidate and enhance the national models for elite sport, including important discussions about the role and purpose of elite sport. The Swedish elite sport system, whilst remaining remarkably stable, is hampered by tensions and conflicts, particularly between the NOC (SOK) and the national sport confederation (RF), which have undermined efforts to reform and enhance the Swedish elite sport system. In comparison, Norway experienced a number of significant changes to elite sport during the 1990s and 2010s, largely triggered by the implications of the breakdown of the Soviet Union and changes in the way that sport had been divided along class and ethnic lines. In addition, the bankruptcy of the dominant Finnish sports association and various doping scandals led to strong criticism and a loss of legitimacy for elite sport. Ultimately, the Finnish state reaction was a return to mass sport and the instrumental value of sport to the welfare of the Finnish population. The authors add to this a discussion about the differences and similarities in organisational models of elite sport across the four nations, assessing the role of the volunteer movement, the degree of unification of national sports and the legitimacy of sport elites, as set out below:

Norway: strong, broad voluntary movement; highly unified structure, high legitimacy of elite sport; centralised authority (support focussed on funding, project support, expertise, active intervention, training centre)

Denmark: strong, broad voluntary movement; highly unified structure, high/ medium legitimacy of elite sport although contested; centralised authority (support focussed on funding, project support, expertise)

Sweden: strong, broad voluntary movement; no unified structure, legitimacy of elite sport contested; segmented structure

Finland: strong, broad voluntary movement; weak unified structure, weak legitimacy of elite sport; segmented, decentralised structure

Interestingly, given that the paper is based upon a most similar systems perspective, the authors conclude by drawing out examples of how the divergence in the organisation and development of elite sport across the Nordic region runs counter to the assumptions that one might have based upon the pattern of political and societal norms in each of the four countries, as set out in the table below:

Country	Socio-political characteristics	Elite sport characteristics
Denmark	State reluctance to intervene	Strong role of state in elite sport
Finland	Strong tradition of centralisation	Highly decentralised elite sport system
Norway	Decentraliation of authority Dislike of elites	Highly centralised elite sport system High degree of legitimacy for elite sport
Sweden	Known for ability to modernise Reacts strongly to international trends	Status quo – preserves current elite sport system Reproduces political divides

This case provides an apposite example of how a particular selection strategy (MSSD in this case) may be used to examine similar cases, predicated on social, political, economic and cultural features to show how despite these similarities, there exist many differences that are unique to each country and run counter to what we may assume based on what we know about the socio-political norms of each country. In this way, Andersen and Ronglan's paper demonstrates the utility of the MSSD approach and reveals that the characteristics of elite sport do not always mirror the nation's dominant socio-political norms.

CHAPTER 5

Ensuring Construct, Sample and Functional Equivalence

Chapter objectives

- To define the concept of equivalence;
- To describe construct, sampling, and functional equivalence issues within sport;
- To suggest potential strategies for researchers to ensure that equivalence is appropriately addressed within comparative research.

The concept of equivalence is a complex and multi-faceted issue. While it is important for all social scientists to understand the concept of equivalence, it should be a central concern of all comparative research. Simply put, if comparative research is about comparing the similarities and differences between two or more phenomena, the issue of equivalence (and its various forms) is about ensuring that the social entities and instruments utilised to compare them are comparable. In other words, it is about making sure that the concepts and instruments employed by researchers to make comparisons in one context are the same when compared in another context. Equivalence is therefore about ensuring that the same phenomenon is being studied across different social units (nations) and that the similarities and differences observed do not refer to fundamentally different things (Baistow, 2000; Davidov et al., 2014; Hantrais, 2009; Johnson, 1998; Jowell, 1998; Landman & Carvalho, 2017; Mills et al., 2006; Mullen, 1995; Øyen, 1990, 2004; Przeworski & Teune, 1966, 1970; Schuster, 2007; Stegmueller, 2011; Van Deth, 2006).

This chapter explores the concept of equivalence and its various forms and elaborates on how issues of equivalence can occur when attempting to make comparisons in sport. The chapter gives attention to three main types of issues related to equivalence issues that are especially relevant to making comparisons within the sporting domain: construct, sample and functional equivalence.

Before we proceed with a discussion of these different types of equivalence, two important caveats should be noted. First, perhaps unsurprisingly by this point, there are fundamental philosophical disagreements about how to ensure equivalence because a researcher's viewpoint on equivalence is largely dependent upon their philosophical assumptions (see chapter 2). Broadly speaking, these differences can be understood as either those who adopt a *nomothetic* approach that focuses on generating theories and concepts that can be applied universally (etic), or an *ideographic* approach, suggesting that this is simply not possible as it is too contextual and culturally specific (emic) (Hofstede, 1998; Przeworski & Teune, 1966). Importantly, the assumptions underpinning research and the methodological approach taken will lead to fundamentally different viewpoints on a) the extent and nature of issues of equivalency and b) the potential strategies that could be used to ensure better equivalency.

In discussing the issue of equivalence, Landman and Carvalho (2017) identified three broad positions: *universalist, relativist* and the *'middle position'*. The *universalist* viewpoint argues that to be able to make meaningful comparisons, the concepts and variables employed must be able to travel analytically and have universal applicability. *Relativists* argue that all meaning is locally constructed and determined, and therefore, any attempt to make comparative claims across nations is limited, if not impossible. The *middle position*, as the name suggests, believes there is a middle ground whereby the instruments employed can be adapted to be more culturally sensitive to ensure that equivalent and meaningful comparisons can be made. Landman and Carvalho's (2017) distinctions are useful here as they demonstrate how general philosophical issues regarding the nature of comparative research translate into specific methodological concerns such as equivalence.

In this sense, parallels can be drawn between Landman and Carvalho's distinctions and Øyen's (1990) typology discussed in the introduction. *Universalists* (or *totalists*) see no difference between comparative sociology and any other form of sociological inquiry, while *relativists* (or *pragmatists/comparativists*) believe that issues of comparative analysis should be embraced and better understood to enable the development of more, culturally sensitive, instruments to compare nations. The difference between Øyen's typology and Landman and Carvalho's distinctions is that the former refers to a general stance on whether or not it is possible to compare nations, and the latter is focused more specifically on the comparability of theoretical concepts and the instruments employed (namely equivalence). As touched on above, these distinctions are largely dictated by one's underlying philosophical position.

The second caveat is that despite the concept's centrality and importance to comparative research, terms to discuss equivalence related issues are used in different ways by different scholars, and are often employed interchangeably. This has resulted in the usage of the term becoming confused and convoluted. As Johnson (1998, p. 2) argues, "perhaps in no field of inquiry, though, has this seemingly elementary concept been assigned as many alternative meanings and disaggregated into as many components as in the field of cross-cultural research". In support of this viewpoint, Johnson (1998) goes on to identify no less than *52 ways* in which the concept of equivalence has been employed across several disciplines, including anthropology, business, sociology and political science.[1] As a result of this continued muddled usage of nomenclature, there are no universally agreed-upon definitions and distinctions between types of equivalence, or possible strategies that can be employed to ensure it. Despite this issue, there does appear to be some broad congruence regarding the essence and nature of equivalence within comparative analysis in general, and there have been many proposals for potential strategies that can be used to ensure better equivalence.

What follows is an attempt to identify some of the most common types of equivalence that are of particular concern and relevance to comparative analysis within the context of sport, as well as a discussion of potential strategies that can be used to ensure better equivalence.

CONSTRUCT EQUIVALENCE

Construct equivalence is about ensuring that concepts and instruments measure the same variables across different cases (countries). In this sense, the notion of construct equivalence is defined here in a similar way to what Johnson (1998) describes more generally as *interpretive equivalence,* in that comparative researchers need to ensure that there is a similarity of meaning between concepts. If the main aim of comparative analysis is to search for similarities and differences between nations, it is important to deploy concepts and instruments that measure equivalent variables across all cases. The essence of construct equivalence is captured in a rhetorical question posed by Przeworski and Teune (1966): "How can valid comparisons be made in cross-national research when so many terms and concepts differ in their meanings from country to county?" (p. 551). The authors go on to argue that "the critical problem in cross-national research is that of identifying 'equivalent' phenomena and analysing the relationships between them in an 'equivalent' fashion" (p. 553). The notion of ensuring equivalent concepts in general, and the specific question posed by Przeworski and Teune (1966), is a frequent and understandable challenge for comparative researchers, as the social units and variables of one context are not always equal and equivalent in another.

---

1   Johnson (1998) notes in his comprehensive review of equivalence within cross-national survey research that many variations of equivalence often "have not been well defined", and that there is considerable overlap between concepts. In his review, the author divides these types of equivalence into two fundamental domains: interpretive and procedural, with the former referring to the similarity of meaning between concepts and the latter measurement and procedure.

The notion of construct equivalence can be understood through some illustrative examples. Consider seemingly comparable and taken-for-granted concepts that you would assume to have equivalence between different countries, but they do not. A simple (albeit a personal and meta-philosophical) question such as 'do you believe in God?' can be interpreted in several ways in different contexts and is therefore quite ambiguous. Indeed, asking this question will produce considerable variance in responses between individuals and/or countries, but how can you ensure that the variance between or within nations can be attributed to the independent variable?

Let's consider the potential variance in the response to the question, 'do you believe in God?' The individual response to the question could be a recognition of either an acceptance of a higher being (monotheist), or multiple beings (polytheist), or an affiliation with a religious group (e.g., Christianity, Mormonism), or sub-group (e.g., Catholicism, Fundamentalism), or the general recognition of belonging to a particular social group (Przeworski & Teune, 1966). Similarly, another example might be the usage of the political spectrum to compare the political orientations of two countries. The commonly understood concept of the political spectrum typically depicts extreme positions such as communism on the left and fascism on the right. Political scientists have often criticised the simplicity of the political spectrum, as it does not sufficiently encapsulate the significant variation that exists within political systems. The political spectrum might be appropriate and make sense in certain countries, but in others there is no equivalent or similar meaning. It could, therefore, be inappropriate or not possible to understand the political leanings of a given sample population through a singular question of whether an individual (or group) is politically either left- or right-leaning, for example.

There are several other similar, potentially non-equivalent, concepts within the context of sport. The obvious and most commonly used terms such as sport, physical activity, participation, sport development/management, coaching, legacy, disability and so on, often have different meanings to different people, and mean different things in different contexts. Even the concept of elite sport itself has varied meanings within different contexts. The commonly held assumption made by many comparative sport policy/management scholars is that elite (or high performance sport) is defined as the pursuit of medal success at World Championships or Olympic and Paralympic Games (De Bosscher et al., 2006, 2015; Green & Houlihan, 2005). Some scholars, however, have adopted a broader definition of elite sport to mean anything above recreational or participation sport. What might be elite for one country can be a different level of achievement for another. To illustrate the problem of inconsistent definitions, in the United Kingdom, UK Sport, the governmental agency responsible for high performance sport, primarily funds sports that are part of the Olympic/Paralympic programme, and athletes who have the potential to medal (podium or podium potential athletes). In this regard, there may be many professional athletes who are either not predicted to produce medal success or are in non-Olympic/Paralympic-based sports, who are therefore not deemed to be elite under the UK Sport national governing body classification and prioritisation system. This could be compared to many other countries who might consider an athlete who is a national champion and not likely to produce medal success as being at the very top of the sport development pyramid, and therefore considered elite. A further example is evident when comparing U.S. sport to other nations. Here, Division I college sport (especially among sports such as American football, basketball, track & field) is largely considered elite. In contrast, college sport in the majority of national contexts is not. In short, like many concepts within social sciences, the term 'elite' is contestable, as it is socially constructed relative to the specific contextual conditions that influenced its construction. These definitional issues matter when asking seemingly simple questions such as: how many elite athletes does a country have? What support is provided to elite athletes? How much government funding is allocated to elite sport?

According to Johnson (1998), "a measure can be identified as having [construct equivalence] to the degree that it exhibits a consistent theoretically-driven pattern of relationships with other variables across the cultural groups being examined" (p. 9). To use another sporting example, if we decide to compare the construct of sport development or coaching between two countries, how do we know and how can we actually say with any certainty that we are identifying the same patterns of relationships within both contexts? Do both countries assume the same understanding and set of social behaviours that we might call sport development or coaching? Equally, there can be as much *intra*-variation as *inter*-variation in the usage of a construct. For example, coaching can mean a completely different thing to different social groups, such as business executives (life coaching) compared to an athlete (sport coaching). Similarly, sport development can be taken to simply represent the joining of the words, as is generally the case in the U.S. Or, it can be viewed to represent an entire field of structures and professionals that are seeking to achieve demonstrable sporting and social outcomes, as is the case in the UK.

One of the most commonly identified issues relating to construct equivalence within the comparative literature is language (Øyen, 1990; Jowell, 1998; Przeworski & Teune, 1966). This is also referred to as *translation equivalence,* whereby the same items measure the same constructs across different cases (Mullen, 1995). For example, despite the vast array of different languages, it is often taken for granted that words are equivalently used across all cultures. Firstly, quite often this is not the case; there are many words in certain languages that have different meanings in different contexts or have no equivalent at all. To illustrate, the word *"awkward"* has no equivalent in Italian; *"shallow"* has no equivalent in French; and the German word *"kummerspeck"* roughly translates to extra weight one puts on after emotional eating, often due to sorrow. In short, there are many words and phrases that do not have exact or like-for-like equivalents.

Second, non-equivalence of language is not isolated to different languages. Construct equivalence issues can be evident between even the closest of matched languages. For example, many comparative studies erroneously assume that the English language is used consistently across English-speaking nations such as the U.S., Canada and the UK. One only has to consider the numerous idiosyncrasies between U.S. English and British English to appreciate the potential limitations of this approach. Consider the differences between normal, everyday concepts which utilise different words for the same object (e.g., car park and parking lot; pavement and sidewalk; holiday and vacation; football and soccer). These different words can also translate to differences in meanings to similar or close substitutable phenomena (e.g., shop vs. store; pants vs. trousers) but some are more fundamental differences that could potentially result in social embarrassment (e.g., chips vs. fries; rubber vs. eraser). A potential consequence of erroneously assuming native English-speaking equivalence is that comparative researchers often do not translate their instruments from one country to another, and therefore run the inherent risk of accidentally deploying non-equivalent concepts within their analysis and attributing observed differences to non-equivalence.

In this sense, although the above sporting and non-sporting examples and the idiosyncrasies of non-equivalent language between U.S. and British English might seem anecdotal, they serve to highlight a potentially important – if not fundamental – equivalence issue that, "different languages are not just equivalent means of defining and communicating the same ideas and concepts. In many respects, they reflect different thought processes, institutional frameworks, and underlying values" (Jowell, 1998, p. 170).

On the basis that comparative researchers face a potential problem of construct equivalence, how should the concept be understood and what potential strategies can be put in place to overcome or mitigate this issue? To begin to understand the concept, it is important to recognise that the issue of concept equivalence is both a social-context specific and empirical issue. For example, does the concept of sport participation mean the same thing in the U.S. as it does in Japan? Does the concept of specialist sport schools in Germany equate to the same thing in India? Whether the concepts of sport participation and specialist sport schools are equivalent depends on the specific countries in question and can only be determined through empirical investigation or at least in-depth knowledge of the specific country.

Furthermore, equivalent concepts are not necessarily the same as identical concepts. As a starting point to ensure better construct equivalence, it may well be inappropriate and/or erroneous to assume that the same concepts should be employed to make comparisons across all social units (nations). To overcome the problem of concept equivalence, comparative researchers might need to go beyond the identification of a 'one-size-fits-all' approach to find similar, matched, like-for-like or 'equivalent indicators' (Przeworski & Teune, 1966). What are considered specialist sport schools in one country, for example, might be more accurately reflected in a broader conceptualisation of education and sport, high school sport, sport academies, or some other equivalent indicator.

Another potential strategy to overcome the issue of non-equivalence of concepts is to employ a set of indicators or measurements, rather than single items (Przeworski & Teune, 1966). This ensures that any variance between countries can be appropriately attributed to the independent variable in question, rather than a misunderstanding or misappropriation of a non-equivalent concept. On this point, Przeworski and Teune (1966, p. 556) argue that "although complete equivalence is probably never possible, attempts can be made to measure equivalence if they are based on a set of indicators or observations". Even if a difference between nations is incorrectly attributed to non-equivalence in concepts, then it should be the case that this relationship holds for some nations (i.e., non-equivalent) and not others. Consequently, the researcher can identify the compounding or intervening variables that may be influencing the observed outcomes.

In responding specifically to the issue of ensuring equivalence in language, researchers can follow procedures and guidelines on how to translate concepts and instruments from one country to another. There are examples of this from the elite sport policy/management literature. De Bosscher et al. (2015), translated their survey instruments and inventories into twelve different languages in order to respond to the issue of non-equivalence of language. More specifically, they developed a comprehensive modus operandi for their SPLISS 2.0 studies with explicitly articulated definitions of key terms such as elite athlete, coach and performance director (pp. 62-63) and noted, where possible, key terms within their inventories in an attempt to reduce non-equivalence of constructs (see case study below for a full elaboration on this study and the strategies that were employed by the researchers to ensure equivalence). Interestingly, despite its importance, there appear to be very few comparative sport studies that explicitly discuss the issue of equivalence or the issue of language and translation equivalence.

SAMPLE EQUIVALENCE

In addition to construct equivalence, comparative researchers need to make sure that their samples are equivalent (Ebbinghaus, 2005; Hantrais, 2009; Jowell, 1998; Kohn, 1987; Øyen, 1990; Schuster, 2007). Sample equivalence involves making decisions on which countries to include and why. As sampling was discussed at length in the previous chapter, it is not necessary to revisit these arguments in full. Nonetheless, two important interrelated points can be drawn from the previous chapter that are pertinent to the present discussion. The first relates to the general sample approach adopted and the second is how these general approaches lead to more specific assumptions about the selected sample.

The decision on sample size – and by extension sample equivalence – should be informed by the approach adopted, i.e., a variable-oriented or case-oriented approach. Any attempt to ensure sample equivalence relates directly to the general approach adopted by the researcher to select countries to make comparisons. The extent and type of sample equivalence issues recognised by a comparative researcher are largely dependent upon their underlying philosophical assumptions and whether a variable-oriented (large-N) or a case-oriented (small-N) approach has been adopted. The issue of sample equivalence is especially challenging for comparative researchers as it requires that there is enough similarity between the comparable entities that comparisons can be made, but also requires sufficient difference that variations can be found through the identification of explanatory factors.

The adoption of either a variable- or case-oriented approach leads to more specific assumptions about the sample and sampling procedure. For example, the selection of cases for those that adopt a variable-oriented approach is often erroneously assumed to be randomised. As discussed in the previous chapter, the selection of countries for comparative inquiry is rarely entirely random, with cases often selected due to practicalities, feasibility or for historical reasons (Ebbinghaus, 2005). As a result of this shortcoming, it is difficult to say whether the sample selected is entirely equivalent or not. Both variable- and case-oriented approaches assume that it is at least theoretically possible to select nations from a sample population. The difference between the approaches is that variable-oriented studies treat the sample as being the same (i.e., homogenous) and seek a randomised selection from the entire possible sample that could be selected (sample population), whereas case-oriented approaches assume that cases are heterogeneous and therefore the selection of cases from the sample population should be made deliberately and purposefully.

In reality, both approaches face significant practical difficulties in being able to achieve either an entirely randomly or purposefully selected sample from any given population. For instance, as variable-oriented approaches treat all cases the same, they should (in theory) – be based on the statistical rules of random selection and randomisation – have an equal chance of being selected. In practice, far from being entirely random, it is more likely that comparative variable-oriented researchers erroneously assume that their sample is randomly selected, when in fact it has most likely been selected in a pseudo-random manner based on meeting certain explicit or implicit criteria. These are usually practicality/feasibility criteria such as the ability to access the data, inclusion in pre-existing datasets, ability to secure appropriate support in host countries, preference or potential bias towards more economically developed countries and so on.

If this occurs, the sample selection is at best most likely to be pseudo-randomised or at worst unknowingly stratified if it is based on criteria – whether it was intended or unintended. The consequence is that researchers assume that they have an equivalent sample, when in reality they do not. Ebbinghaus (2005, p. 136) describes this as the "illusion of random sampling" which in turn can lead to the problem of contingency. The danger here is that cases can be deliberately or inadvertently selected based on providing a positive outcome (known as selection bias) which can potentially lead to results in false inferences being made – see chapter 4 on sample selection for a more detailed discussion of this issue.

There are many ways for comparative researchers to guard against the problem of sampling equivalence. The most obvious ones are to ensure that comparative researchers provide a clear articulation of their own philosophical position and their general orientation including consciously thinking about, and being aware of, their own assumptions relating to sampling. To avoid the *'too many variables, not enough countries'* scenario, it is important to ensure that the sample selected is appropriate for the number of variables employed. In this sense, comparative researchers should resist the temptation to add as many countries or use as many variables as possible and only use enough cases as needed to achieve the desired outcomes. It is partly for this reason that Jowell (1998, p. 175) suggests that "cross-national surveys should ideally be confined to the smallest number of countries consistent with their aims rather than celebrating as many nations as possible in their purview".

FUNCTIONAL EQUIVALENCE

In addition to overcoming construct and sample equivalence issues, comparative researchers also have to ensure that the data collected and analysed has functional or measurement equivalence (Davidov et al., 2014; Dogan & Pelassy, 1990; Ebbinghaus, 2005; Hantrais, 2009; Johnson, 1998; Jowell, 1998; Landman & Carvalho, 2017; Mullen, 1995; Øyen, 1990, 2004; Schuster, 2007; Stegmueller, 2011). Precise definitions of functional equivalence are difficult to discern from the comparative literature, but the notion is understood here in its broadest sense, along similar lines to that described by Dogan and Pelassy (1990) as well as incorporating what Johnson (1998) labelled *procedural equivalence,* which involves ensuring equivalence in methods, measurement and procedure. In distinguishing functional equivalence from the previous two issues of equivalence, functional equivalence refers to more fundamental issues about whether the variables identified and the measures employed throughout the research design process are standardised between countries. The focus here is on the apparatus and data used and whether they can be used to meaningfully compare. The essence of this issue is that just because data could be used for comparative purposes does not mean that they should be used. Equally, not all comparative data are appropriate for comparative analysis. As Schuster (2007, p. 99) notes, "comparable data are not necessarily usable data, but neither are usable data necessarily comparable data".

Jowell (1998) outlines the nature of functional equivalence for comparative researchers when discussing the deployment of survey instruments. He suggests, "a great deal of work in national surveys goes into the sheer process of attaining standardization, or equal treatment of respondents and potential respondents and of different classes of respondents. Only to the extent that a national survey succeeds in these goals are its findings likely to approximate some sort of reality" (p. 169). Although Jowell's remarks are specifically about the usage of cross-national surveys, the quote serves to highlight more generally the extent of the challenge for comparative researchers in ensuring functional or measurement equivalence.

Several issues can be subsumed under the banner of functional equivalence, and as such the reader is directed elsewhere for a more detailed treatment of each of these issues (Davidov et al., 2014; Dogan & Pelassy, 1990; Johnson, 1998; Mullen, 1995; Øyen, 1990; Schuster, 2007; Stegmueller, 2011). As previously stated, there is no common agreement regarding exactly what constitutes functional equivalence. Nonetheless, two major functional equivalence issues can be drawn from the comparative literature: one broad and one specific.

The broader issue relates to the identification of functionally equivalent social units or institutions (e.g., government, parliament, sport, education) and the implications of this for how comparative studies are approached, emphasising a more conceptual and theoretical concern. To explain this issue, it is worth taking a step back to consider the basic notion of *function*. Here, function can be understood as a natural purpose of something or why something exists. The idea of having functional equivalence stems from the theory of functionalism and the notion that different parts of society, such as the elements of an elite sport system, for example, exist to perform a particular function (Dogan & Pelassy, 1990). Functionalism is often explained by – and by extension, functional equivalence can be understood through – an analogy of the human body in that different parts of the body exist to perform a particular function. The heart is a muscle that pumps blood around the body, the lungs take in and expel air, the kidney filters blood and so on. Regardless of what species you are observing, it is possible, at least in theory, to identify the organ from the function that it performs, even if they might be different in shape and size. One does not have to see the same heart to know that it is a heart from identifying its key features and functionality within the body.

The common assumption made by those seeking to compare is that they presume that because the same entities with the same names can be identified, they must be equivalent. This is not always the case, as not only can the same entities perform different functions, but also different entities can perform the same functions. On this point, Dogan and Pelassy (1990) argue that, "the same performance may be accomplished in various countries by different [entities] and similar or comparable institutions may fulfil, in various countries, different tasks" (p. 37). The key point here is that different structures within countries might perform the same function, and equally the same structures can perform different functions. In both cases, there can be a potential lack of functional equivalence. This point can be illustrated further through considering the roles, responsibilities and structures of government, the cabinet and parliament. Within the UK, these entities refer to the people with authority to govern, the elected members who are given portfolios of responsibility through departments (e.g., the Department of Education or the Department of Digital, Culture, Media and Sport), and the elected representatives (members of parliament) from different constituencies around the country. In some countries, however, these functions are performed by different entities or through collaboration. In the U.S., for example, Congress performs many of the functions of a parliament, such as holding the government to account and legislating. In this way, these differing systems share some level of functional equivalence, although importantly, each national system has structural features and cultural characteristics that make each unique and different to that which they are compared.

This issue can be directly applied to the sporting context. Regarding elite sport systems, for example, it may be possible to identify the same structures or entities that perform the same function. In both Canada and the UK, for example, funding comes directly from governmental agencies through the exchequer (taxpayer) and national lottery funds. The non-departmental public bodies of UK Sport and Own the Podium, the governmental agencies responsible for overseeing and funding high performance sport in the respective countries, can therefore generally be considered to be functionally equivalent. Equally, there are examples in elite sport systems whereby the same functions are performed by different actors. Some countries such as Poland have no high performance government agency equivalent because the National Olympic Committee assumes responsibility for the allocation of government funding. In this case, it can be argued that both government agencies and the National Olympic Committees, although different organisational entities, share some level of functional equivalence.

In recognising this issue, a comparative researcher must ensure that the entities identified for analysis have the same function in order to make meaningful comparisons. Researchers must also be careful when choosing which entities to compare, as the same entity in one nation does not necessarily equate to being functionally equivalent to the other. It may be necessary to study different entities in different contexts and investigate them in-depth to understand their roles and responsibilities to be able to claim functional equivalence, as well as being transparent about any distinct or differing features. This requires considerable conceptualising and potential methodological adjustment to ensure equivalence. It is for these reasons that many comparative scholars strongly recommend that researchers have knowledge of, and are situated within, the national research contexts in which comparisons are being made, as they are the experts regarding whether the entities being studied have functional equivalence.

The more specific issue of functional equivalence relates to the deployment of instruments, measures and procedures that are used to ensure equivalent responses. Some scholars have termed this form of equivalence as *measurement equivalence* (Mullen, 1995). This essentially seeks to address the question of whether the same measurements and apparatus hold across different countries. Issues regarding this sub-category of functional equivalence relate to: (i) whether the questions employed have functional equivalence; (ii) whether the responses to the questions provided have functional equivalence; and (iii) whether the data collected and analysed have functional equivalence (Dogan & Pelassy, 1990; Johnson, 1998; Mullen, 1995; Øyen, 1990). Each of these questions and their associated issues of functional/measurement equivalence will be discussed in turn.

Regarding whether the questions employed have functional/measurement equivalence, it is worth considering the obvious examples of measures that are different between nations – what is Celsius in one country could be Fahrenheit in another, miles versus kilometres per hour, dollars vs. euros or even US dollars and Canadian dollars. In much the same way as you might decide to exchange currency or buy a power converter before you go on holiday, the questions within the instruments used to compare should also be converted to the measurements of the country in question. This is sometimes referred to as *calibration equivalence* because it involves the calibration of measurements to enable comparisons (Mullen, 1995). There is also a clear overlap between this sub-type of functional equivalence and concept equivalence with the distinction being the former relating to ensuring the appropriate procedural measures are being employed, and the latter equivalence with regards to the concepts utilised within these instruments. An example of the problem of calibration equivalence exists in Play the Game's National Sport Observer. The National Sport Observer seeks to measure the extent to which National Governing Bodies of Sport (NGBs) meet principles of good governance. The measure includes a bank of over 270 indicators, developed by European researchers. Despite claims that the indicators have international relevance, the measure includes a number of indicators which fail to recognise the different national contexts. For example, indicator 6.1 focuses on the production of an annual report. Annual reports within NGBs of sport may be common in Europe, but they are non-existent in the U.S. context. Indicator 13.1 asks about the representation of the general assembly. Again, though such structures are common across Europe, they do not exist in the U.S.. In contrast, indicator 6.6 asks whether the annual report gives clear attention to the finances of the organisation. In the U.S. context, NGBs of sport are required to post their annual IRS financial return, with clear details of income and expenditure. Thus, meeting or not meeting these three examples, in the U.S. context at least, says little about good governance and rather more about how well the measure fits with the local context. The Sport Governance

Observer enables these issues to be addressed by entering a score of non-applicable. However, such entries deviate from the overall exercise of measuring good governance as the indicator is essentially exempted from the measure, rather than being adapted to more sensitively consider local circumstances. One way in which these issues can be more sensitively addressed is the use of local researchers who are familiar with the empirical context in question and can therefore adapt the measure to fit the local context.

Another functional equivalence issue centres on whether the responses to the questions employed are comparable across cases. Mullen (1995) identifies two potential threats to this sub-type of equivalence when employing survey instruments: familiarity with scaling and scoring methods, and response bias. In terms of familiarity with scaling and scoring, some researchers, countries or contexts may not be as familiar with these types of research methodological approaches, which may pose a potential threat to reliability. Also, responses might be different between countries depending on their social norms or culture. Some countries may, in general, be more confident and outspoken whilst others value humility. The outcome of these socio-cultural differences may result in different responses to the questions posed. These issues might be spotted through the identification of inconsistencies in responses or tendencies towards the mean (which usually occurs in times of uncertainty). Also, researchers can check that there is no systematic bias in response to questions. If this is the case, it is likely to indicate functional equivalence issues. Mullen (1995) and Johnson (1998) recommend a number of empirical techniques that can be used to check for functional equivalence.

Another functional equivalence issue relates to whether the data collected and analysed have functional equivalence. This is commonly the case when only a small number of questions are employed that encapsulate a particular variable under investigation. A solution to this issue is to ensure that multiple indicators are used to measure or capture each variable. This ensures that the variance in response from the data collected is reflective of the observed differences. The issue of data collection equivalence also relates to more practical considerations of what primary or secondary data are available to support comparisons. For primary data, this is often a feasibility and data access issue and a trade-off between cost and resources, and the ability to include countries. For secondary data, this issue relates to whether the data that exist are appropriate for comparisons and, if so, whether they should be used for comparative inquiry.

The problem of functional or measurement equivalence in general, and the issue of data collection equivalence specifically, appears to be particularly applicable to the sport policy/management domain given that much of the elite sport policy/management literature draws heavily upon secondary data sources to make comparisons. An example from the sporting context is the usage of national participation survey data (e.g., Active Lives Survey – Sport England; Sport Participation Survey – Canadian Heritage; Sport

Participation Survey – National Sport Goods Association [U.S.]). To make national data sets fully functionally equivalent they need to be completely standardised. At times, the quality and utility of these types of data sets are questionable in their own right. They are designed for completely different purposes, employ fundamentally different methodologies, and produce different metrics that arguably make comparisons meaningless. It is not possible, for example, to directly compare the UK-based Active Lives Survey with the Canadian Sport Participation Survey or the U.S. Sport Participation Survey, as all three have different scopes/purposes and employ significantly different methodologies. In short, they have no functional equivalence, with the problem further compounded by a lack of construct equivalence.

The usage of these secondary data sources is often due to pragmatic reasons, but also because they are the only, or the best, data sets available. Furthermore, very few sport studies have explicitly addressed and/or adopted measures to ensure that the entities studied are functionally equivalent. There are even fewer sport-related studies that have conducted preliminary empirical tests to ensure that the instruments and apparatus employed have equivalence. One exception from the elite sport policy/management domain is De Bosscher et al. (2015), who partly attempted to address this functional equivalence issue by drawing upon larger (or at least as large possible) comparative data sets. De Bosscher et al. (2015), adopted the International Social Survey Programme (ISSP) and the Eurobarometer (EB) survey to standardise sport participation. These efforts are, however, rare with very few sport scholars explicitly discussing how (if at all) they have ensured functional equivalence. See the case study below for a full elaboration on the strategies employed by De Bosscher and colleagues to ensure equivalence.

There is a clear overlap between functional equivalence and conceptual equivalence, with the former relating to how particular concepts are utilised for comparative purposes, and the latter denoting how to ensure equivalent entities are being compared and measurements deployed. Furthermore, it is apparent that functional equivalence has an additional temporal dimension, in that this issue can occur at many stages of the research process. Przeworski and Teune (1966), suggest that functional equivalence issues can arise at both the data collection and data analysis stages of the research process. Johnson (1998), on the other hand, proposes several potential strategies for ensuring functional equivalence at four phases of the research process: question development phase, pre-testing phase, data collection phase and data analysis phase. Regardless of which stages these issues are identified and mitigated by comparative researchers, it is necessary to recognise that issues of functional equivalence can arise at any point in the research process. It is therefore important that researchers build in strategies throughout the research process to ensure better functional equivalence. While Johnson (1998) and Mullen (1995) provide a comprehensive list of potential functional equivalence strategies, this chapter has touched on some of the most common strategies, including: translating survey instruments, utilising local researchers, empirically testing for equivalence, checking for inconsistencies and using multiple indicators.

CHAPTER SUMMARY

This chapter has outlined the concept of equivalence and its various forms and provided some potential strategies for ensuring better equivalence. In particular, it has delineated three types of equivalence: construct, sample and functional equivalence, and highlighted a number of potential strategies within each that can be employed to ensure better equivalence. A summary of the potential strategies identified in this chapter is presented in Table 5.1. It is important to note that this summary table is intended to be illustrative rather than exhaustive and for a more comprehensive discussion of these strategies the reader is directed elsewhere (Davidov et al. 2014; Johnson, 1998; Mullen, 1995; Øyen, 1990; Stegmueller, 2011).

Table 5.1 Potential strategies for improving equivalence

Construct equivalence	Sample equivalence	Functional equivalence
Define concepts/terms	Clear articulation of inclusion/exclusion criteria	Use researchers with local knowledge of the national context
Identification of equivalent indicators	Clear articulation of research design (MSSD/MDSD)	Use standardised data sets
Usage of multiple indicators	Ensure sample selection is proportional to variables employed	Standardise data (if not standardised)
Translate and retranslate instruments	Randomise sample (large-N only)	Use empirical techniques, e.g., confirmatory factor analysis
Translation of native-speaking instruments	Avoid selection bias, i.e., choosing cases to support a positive outcome	Use primary data where possible
Adoption of clear and transparent translation protocols and procedures	Openly acknowledge and recognise limitations	Data triangulation
Empirically test equivalency of concepts		Check for inconsistent responses

The issue of equivalence can be understood in a much similar fashion to how researchers ensure appropriate research quality through consideration of the validity and reliability of their projects (Bryman, 2015; Guba & Lincoln, 1984). For comparative researchers, the issue of equivalence is an additional layer of consideration in the research design that is required when attempting to carry out social inquiry. Ensuring equivalence is especially important, if not central, to the overall purpose of the research. Without ensuring equivalence, the study is indeterminate because it is not possible to attribute the findings of a study with the similarities and differences observed. Without equivalence, any attempt to generate or test theory becomes incommensurable.

In building upon the final point regarding functional equivalence, what can collectively be drawn from the above discussion, and comparative literature in general, is the need to build in strategies to ensure better equivalence throughout the research process. The choice of wording in regards to 'better' equivalence is deliberate here in that quite to what extent it is practically possible to achieve what Verba et al. (1978) described as "complete equivalence" – the hypothetical and unobtainable achievement of total equivalence, i.e., complete construct, sample and functional equivalence, seems an unlikely if not impossible task. This seems a rather impractical (albeit helpful) standard in which to enhance the practice of comparative research within sport. As Dogan and Pelassy (1990, p. 16) note, what comparative researchers "should seek is not paralyzing perfection, but the most satisfying approximation to it". For this reason, it is argued that the best that comparative researchers can hope to achieve is something closer to total equivalence to enable less imperfect comparisons of approximations of social reality to be made.

Another general consideration is that although some of the potential strategies identified above may be useful, they could understandably be perceived as being quite difficult or practically unrealistic to incorporate into a comparative research design. It is argued here, as it has been suggested elsewhere, that although equivalence is of central concern to comparative researchers, "it should be noted that not all forms of equivalence are necessarily created equal" (Johnson, 1998, p. 30). Quite to what extent say, construct equivalence is more important than sampling equivalence, is beyond the scope of this particular chapter. Nonetheless, it is appropriate to recognise that it is perhaps not feasible for those who are seeking to make comparisons to employ all of the aforementioned strategies (summarised in Table 5.1). On this basis, the best advice that can be given to those who are seeking to compare sporting nations is "to employ as many of these techniques as possible *within reason*, given that various methodologies may be more appropriate to one specific form of equivalence or another" (Johnson, 1998, p. 31). Assuming that it is not possible to achieve total or complete equivalence, it is recommended that comparative researchers adopt the pragmatist position and, at least, attempt to explicitly address the multi-faceted issue of equivalence and do the best they can with the time and resources available.

As a final point, it is perhaps worth considering that even if sport researchers were somehow able to overcome, or at least mitigate, some of the above-identified issues of equivalence, it is equally important to recognise that:

> ...comparative studies, will, of course, always be defeated to some extent by differences between nations in matters or taxonomy and technique. Their very starting point is that important differences exist between nations in their behaviours, circumstances and attitudes. It is hardly surprising, then, that some of the differences should confound the achievement of standardized measures nor that the difficulties tend to increase with the number and heterogeneity of the countries involved (Jowell, 1998, p. 173).

One important takeaway from this chapter is that issues of equivalence are mostly unavoidable. After all, are comparative studies not entirely predicated on the basis that there are different characteristics or features that make them unique and worth comparing in the first place? Seen from this viewpoint, the issues of equivalence are likely to be a constant feature of comparative inquiry and therefore a perennial concern for those attempting to compare sporting nations.

CASE STUDY 5: ENSURING EQUIVALENCE THROUGH THE SPLISS ACCOUNT (DE BOSSCHER AND COLLEAGUES)

The research of De Bosscher and colleagues is perhaps one of the best known examples of comparative studies in elite sport. The project was conceived in 2002 with the creation of a conceptual model of sport policy factors that lead to international sporting success (giving the project its name, SPLISS). The conceptual model was empirically tested as part of the SPLISS phase 1.0 project completed in 2006/7 and involved a total of six nations (Belgium, Canada, Italy, the Netherlands, Norway and the United Kingdom). The primary objective of SPLISS 1.0 was to gain insights into the key factors in elite sport policy and the relationship between these factors and international sporting success. Conceptually, the SPLISS framework consisted of nine pillars representing inputs, throughputs and outputs, and operationalised into a total of 105 critical success factors. Methodologically, the researchers claim that the research is predicated on a mixed-methods approach, consisting of an overall elite sport policy inventory and an elite sport climate survey. The policy inventory was completed using interviews with policy agents and through the analysis of secondary sources such as policy documentation. For each of the nine pillars (detailed in chapter 7), 105 critical success factors were divided into open-ended and closed questions, which were subsequently translated into numerical data to allow for fair comparisons across countries. The purpose of the elite sport climate survey was to measure success indicators as they are perceived by primary users (athletes, coaches and performance directors) in each nation. This survey required primary users to respond to dichotomous (yes/no) and five-point Likert scale (ordinal) questions on each of the nine pillars and 105 critical success factors. The Likert scale responses were calculated by multiplying the response values, where 1.00 = highly developed, 0.75 = sufficiently developed, 0.50 = reasonably developed, 0.25 = insufficiently developed, and 0 = not developed. The sub-factor scores were then totalled for each critical success factor and then aggregated into a total percentage score for each of the nine pillars. The primary output from SPLISS 1.0 was a traffic light scale depicting the relative performance of each nation against 105 critical success factors together with a radar chart showing overall performance across the nine pillars.

While the SPLISS 2.0 project followed a very similar approach, modifications were introduced in order to strengthen the research. First, the primary objective of SPLISS 2.0 was to better understand which sport policies influence international sporting success, how sport policies influence international sporting success, and to obtain better insights into the effectiveness and efficiency of elite sport policies across different nations. The same conceptual framework was applied, with nine pillars, a reduction from 105 critical success factors to 96, and the addition of an explicit 750 sub-factors relating to each of the 96 critical success factors. The study for SPLISS 2.0 was expanded to include a total of 15 nations. Additionally, the SPLISS 2.0 study gave more explicit attention to some of the challenges of comparative work than was presented in SPLISS 1.0. The primary output from SPLISS 2.0 was similar to SPLISS 1.0, although additional statistical methods were used (z-scores, distance from mean, cumulative probability scores) in an attempt to deepen the insights into elite sport systems and the success between pillars and critical success factors.

Clearly, the notion of equivalence is of central importance to the SPLISS project, as it is primarily concerned with using a number of researchers, a number of research participants and a consistent research instrument across a number of differing national contexts in order to compare elite sport policy. In so doing, the SPLISS researchers would want to be confident that they were comparing the same phenomenon in different contexts in order to ensure that their methods were valid, their results accurate and their efforts worthwhile. To enter into such work without addressing equivalence is to accept the fundamental flaw of failing to act on the very differences (by nation) that make the comparative work worthwhile in the first place.

It is clear to see some progress on issues of equivalence with the SPLISS project, just in comparing phase 2.0 with phase 1.0, and the explicit acceptance of major limitations in phase 2.0 that were not as clearly addressed in phase 1.0. Additionally, De Bosscher and colleagues employed other strategies to address the issues of construct and functional equivalence, as follows:

Construct equivalence: defined the key terms/concepts; translated their survey into multiple languages; and utilised local researchers to manage the execution of the project.

Functional equivalence: independent (e.g., Infostrada database) and supra-national (e.g., the Eurobarometer survey) datasets; triangulated data so as to avoid overreliance on one source; prepared detailed work protocols.

Importantly, while such steps represent progress in minimising the effects of non-equivalence, it does not mean that all problems are reduced to the point where they have no adverse impacts on a comparative analysis of national approaches to elite sport (Jowell, 1998). With regards to SPLISS, there remain at least three key problems of non-equivalency:

1. **Construct equivalence:** while the local researchers may assist with issues relating to construct equivalence, they also bring with them a new set of problems relating to inter-observer and study reliability. Despite protocols, this approach leaves each researcher with discretion to assess their own nation's sporting system, thus leaving considerable leeway for researcher bias and the suppression of cultural specificity.

2. **Functional equivalence:** despite steps to minimise the problems of functional equivalence, the SPLISS work remains predicated on estimates of financial inputs as definitions of expenditure (what is included and excluded) and sport delivery mechanisms vary considerably from nation to nation. In this way, it is not possible to know how the inputs of one country compare (in detail) to the inputs of another country.

3. **Sample equivalence:** while SPLISS has developed inclusion criteria, the sample remains largely based on pragmatism. It is a result of nations that are willing

and able to take part in the research project. Unfortunately, the sample does not include nations that dominate the medals or nations that have won no medals at all. Thus, the sample, while convenient, runs the risk of selection bias or 'the problem of contingency' (Ebbinghaus, 2005). Consequently, we end up with a partial picture predicated on data from some, without consideration of the most and least successful nations.

In sum, these problems reflect the challenging nature of equivalence. At best, we can take steps to manage and mitigate the challenges of non-equivalence and, at the same time, avoid the trap of assuming that because we have taken such steps that our work is devoid of equivalence-related problems. If we couple such approaches with awareness and transparency about the limits of our work, we can strengthen the equivalency of our work, openly recognise that some steps are entirely impractical or unachievable, demonstrate a self-awareness of our findings and acknowledge the need for caution in drawing absolute conclusions.

CHAPTER 6

Data Collection, Analysis and Outputs

Chapter objectives

- To discuss practical issues relating to the collection and analysis of comparative data;
- To suggest potential strategies for comparative researchers to overcome/ mitigate *data collection* and *access* related issues;
- To suggest potential strategies for comparative researchers to overcome/ mitigate *analysis* and *output* related issues.

Previous chapters have examined questions regarding why we conduct comparative research and the underlying motivations for comparing sporting nations (Chapters 1-3). They have also discussed various strategies, approaches and methods for conducting comparative inquiry (Chapter 4-5). This chapter focuses on the practical issues faced by comparative researchers when attempting to make comparisons between sporting nations. To reiterate a statement made in the introduction of the book, the purpose here is *not* to provide a step-by-step how-to guide of how comparative research should or should not be carried out. Nor is the purpose of this chapter to provide detailed commentary on, or specific recommendations for, particular approaches that can be adopted to compare sporting nations. Also, it should be noted that many of the issues identified below are not necessarily unique to comparative inquiry. The issues discussed are evident across and within several research disciplines. Nonetheless, it is argued that these issues are particularly pronounced in, and have implications for, the comparative domain. Furthermore, it should be acknowledged that many of the issues identified herein are largely dependent upon the philosophical assumptions and methodological choices of the researcher. Therefore, quite to what extent a researcher deems a practical issue to be a problem or whether a practical issue exists at all is largely dictated by their philosophical leaning and their preferred methodological approach.

This chapter seeks to identify some of the key practical issues relating to the collection, analysis and presentation/output of data relating to comparative inquiry and the potential limitations that comparative researchers might face regardless of the philosophical or methodological approach adopted. These issues include – but are not limited to – case/ participant recruitment, data access restrictions, researcher selection bias, ensuring standardised protocol, issues of time-lag, issues of cross-sectional data, data sensitivity, data overload, funding/resource constraints and dependency, data oversimplification, overstated or indeterminant research findings, and issues related to generalisability of findings to other countries or contexts. These practical issues are summarised in table 6.1.

Table 6.1: Overview of practical issues related to data collection, analysis and outputs of comparative research

Participant recruitment	Time-lag	Data reduction/ oversimplification
Data availability/access restrictions	Cross-sectional data issues	Overstated findings
Researcher selection bias	Data overload	Indeterminant findings
Protocol standardisation issues	Funding/resource constraints	Limited generalisability
Data sensitivity	Funder/stakeholder dependency	

Many of the issues relating to comparative data collection, analysis and output identified herein have, albeit to varying extents, been experienced and addressed by researchers within the elite sport policy/management domain. As such, and consistent with previous chapters, this chapter will draw upon examples from this domain. These examples not only illustrate practical issues, but also identify some of the potential strategies that can be employed to overcome or at least mitigate these concerns. These potential strategies are summarised in table 6.2.

The chapter is organised in the logical sequencing of the research process beginning with issues relating to data collection, access and analysis. This is followed by a discussion of issues relating to data output and presentation, and a broader consideration of how data and findings of comparative studies are presented, and the extent to which they can be generalised across other countries. Interwoven throughout the chapter is a discussion of potential strategies that can be employed by comparative researchers to overcome (or at least mitigate) some of these practical issues.

As will become apparent, many of the practical issues identified herein have considerable overlap with each other and the various stages of the research process. It is acknowledged that the ordering of these issues in a sequential manner is therefore somewhat artificial.

This is why the summary tables of the practical issues (Table 6.1) and potential strategies (Table 6.2) are presented collectively, rather than categorised within specific stages of the research process for example. Nonetheless, discussing issues and potential strategies in this manner provides an appropriate structuring device to identify and discuss the various practical issues faced by comparative researchers seeking to compare sporting nations.

Table 6.2: Potential strategies for overcoming/mitigating practical issues with data collection, analysis and outputs

Utilise multiple data collection strategies	Only analyse comparable data	Avoid oversimplification of data/study findings
Utilise multiple sources of data	Triangulate data	Explicitly acknowledge limitations of knowledge claims
Establish detailed modus operandi	Conduct longitudinal-based studies	Explicitly acknowledge limitations of findings
Shorten data collection period	Utilise and involve local research teams	Explicitly acknowledge limitations of generalisation
Only collect data necessary to achieve goals	Involve local research team throughout the research process	Be cautious/tentative with research findings

DATA COLLECTION – ACCESS AND ANALYSIS

As well as providing a clear justification for the methodological choices made (as discussed in previous chapters), a comparative researcher also faces a range of practical issues related to collecting, accessing and analysing data when attempting to compare sporting nations (Hantrais, 2009; Jowell, 1998; Landman & Carvalho, 2017; Øyen, 1990; Schuster, 2007). These issues include, but are not limited to, participant recruitment, data availability/access issues (quantity and quality), researcher convenience and selection bias, ensuring standardised protocols, data time-lag, cross-sectional data limitations and funding/resource constraints. Each of these issues and their implications will be discussed in turn.

PARTICIPANT (SAMPLE) RECRUITMENT

This practical issue relates to the ability of comparative researchers to find enough social units and to be able to gain access to the participants required to make meaningful comparisons. As demonstrated in Chapter 4 (selecting countries), this issue does depend upon whether a researcher decides to adopt a most similar or most different (MSSD/MDSD) approach to case selection. In both cases, comparative researchers need to identify a number of social units that meet their pre-requisite inclusion/exclusion criteria. The issue of being able to find enough similar or different social units (countries) also depends on the dependent variable sought and what factors the comparative researcher seeks to control for through case selection (Przeworski & Teune, 1970). As also highlighted in Chapter 4, this is often a challenge for comparative researchers as very few (if any) countries are similar (MSSD) or different (MDSD) on all variables apart from the dependent variable in question (Anckar, 2008; Przeworski & Teune, 1970).

Furthermore, comparative analysis, by design, is time- and resource-intensive and requires comparative researchers to collect data from numerous countries often spanning large geographical areas. In addition, comparative researchers often cannot fully separate or detach themselves from their own national context. Even the most accomplished comparative researchers will likely experience the practical difficulty of gaining access to countries and being able to fully understand the socio-historical context and other nuances that exist between them. As a consequence of the nature and type (i.e., specificity and breadth) of information sought for comparative studies, it is likely that those who seek to make comparisons will attempt to formulate a research team of local researchers and/or key informants to carry out their analysis – see discussion below on the implications of this methodological decision. In doing so, comparative researchers are avoiding having to undertake comparative research and interpret data in countries with which they are not familiar (Jowell, 1998).

Utilising local researchers is also a potential strategy for overcoming another access-related issue, namely the issue of being able to gain access to and find enough participants from which to collect data. This is particularly the case when comparing more niche phenomena or having strict inclusion/exclusion criteria for participant selection. Researchers within the sport policy/management domain often rely upon 'elite' interviewing of senior administrators or politicians, or seek to elicit the views of elite athletes or coaches within their respective countries. For example, the analysis by Bergsgard et al. (2007) of policy change drew upon interviews with several senior administors and governmental officials in Canada, England, Germany and Norway. In this case, interviewees were selected on the basis of having an in-depth knowledge of policy and decision-making within sport in their respective countries. Purposefully selecting participants on this basis considerably delimits the number of participants who can be included within the study and makes access to participants difficult. Dowling et al. (2017) highlight this issue in their analysis of the application of comparative models to the Paralympic context. In particular, their analysis highlights the challenge of comparing para-participation with able-bodied athletes, insofar as the potential sample population of Paralympic athletes is likely to be considerably smaller than that found across able-bodied athletes. This not only makes data access increasingly difficult, in that there are fewer Paralympic athletes, but it also runs the potential risk of overstating the differences that may or may not exist between them (i.e., able-bodied and disability) and the countries compared. In response to these data access challenges, in addition to being cautious and tentative about their findings, comparative sport researchers have often developed working partnerships with government sporting agencies as gatekeepers and/or relied upon their professional networks to gain access to these key informants.

DATA ACCESS/AVAILABILITY ISSUES – QUALITY AND QUANTITY

Closely linked to the above issues of participant/sample recruitment is a more general consideration of data access in terms of the quantity and quality of the data collected. In regard to the quantity, and as highlighted in previous chapters, comparative researchers are pragmatic in that they often rely upon and utilise the best available data within their selected countries. Issues regarding data access are particularly apparent when comparative researchers rely upon secondary (i.e., pre-existing) sources of data from the selected countries, such as participation or census data. As has been outlined in previous chapters, quite often pre-existing datasets are non-equivalent in terms of the concepts and the methodology employed (see Chapter 5). Thus, even when comparative researchers can access secondary data, the comparative researcher must assess the extent to which data are useful and can permit meaningful comparisons to be made. The issue of data access is dependent upon the countries being compared, as there are likely to be differences and biases in the availability of data in some countries compared to others (Ebbinghaus, 2005). This issue is closely linked to another practical issue regarding selection bias and the problem of contingency outlined below.

The collection of data for comparative studies is not just an issue of quantity, and the above discussion of data sensitivity and the extent to which participants (vis-à-vis countries) are willing to share detailed information leads us to a broader consideration of the quality of data. Most comparative studies within the sport policy/management domain rely upon a small team of 'local' researchers who are often conveniently based in the countries selected for comparison – an issue which in and of itself may be indicative of pre-selection of cases based upon a particular outcome (see the issue of selection bias/ problem of contingency below). The typical rationale for using local researchers is that they have detailed knowledge and understanding of the country and its socio-cultural, historical and political context in general, and with regards to the sporting landscape specifically. Also, because they are fully immersed in the socio-cultural context of the (sporting) nation, they can therefore act as a conduit between the research team and other countries to translate concepts, gain access to key organisations and agencies, collect data, and help to identify or explain the similarities and differences between nations. On this basis, the use of 'local' researchers is appropriate, understandable and justifiable as it mitigates some of the previously discussed issues relating to equivalence (see Chapter 5).

The practical reality of utilising a single local researcher (or even a small team of local researchers) is that it requires considerable coordination and management of these teams to carry out the research effectively. Each local researcher effectively acts as a conduit that is responsible for representing, translating, accessing and collecting data for an entire nation. This is by no means an easy (or even entirely feasible) task. Consequently, local researchers must be selected carefully in order to ensure that they have both the capability and capacity necessary to carry out the research. Whilst the issue of capability to a large extent requires a judgement call to be made by the research team based on the individual researchers' track-record and competencies, the latter issue of capacity raises more fundamental questions regarding the extent to which individuals and/or countries can, or should, support the implementation of the comparative research process. Not only does this often require the necessary pre-requisite research training and skills to carry out comparative data collection, but it presumes that they have the necessary time and resources to carry out the comparative analysis. This approach assumes, amongst other things, that the research is not centrally funded and that they also follow a similar research tradition and share the same, if not largely similar, philosophical leanings and expertise. In reality, practical limitations often mean that only select nations with sufficient capacity (i.e., time and resources), similar interests and values, and researchers from specific universities and/or organisational agencies, can take part in such large-scale comparative projects.

Another issue relating to data quality stems from the willingness and ability of participants to divulge and share information, particularly sensitive information that could lead to a competitive advantage between sporting nations. Even the most minor of improvements to the development of elite sport systems could, in turn, impact athlete performance and lead to the difference between a gold and a silver medal. Sometimes medals are lost or won by the finest of margins. An example of this issue/tension between wanting to benchmark a nation's performance, but not wanting to lose a competitive edge, is evident from De Bosscher et al.'s (2015) study, whereby the UK chose not to be involved in SPLISS 2.0 as "many nations were looking at the UK as a best practice benchmark and as such the UK felt less eager to take part in SPLISS 2.0" (p. 67). This decision to not be included in the follow-up study may, in part, be because data collection occurred around the preparation and hosting of the London 2012 Olympic Games and key informants (i.e., politicians, governmental officials and professional administrators working for national sport organisations and agencies) may not have wanted politically and operationally sensitive information to be shared with other sporting nations. On this basis, it is plausible (if not highly likely) that any data shared are likely to be described as 'non-critical' information and will probably be presented in a manner that is deliberately vague. Presuming that the data collection is sufficient (albeit general and vague), comparative researchers should at minimum acknowledge the extent to which meaningful comparisons can be made given the limitations identified above.

RESEARCHER CONVENIENCE AND SELECTION BIAS

A third practical issue relates to the non-random selection of countries and researchers based upon practical limitations, such as resource constraints, convenience or researcher bias. Conducting comparative analysis is both time- and resource-intensive and as a result, researchers often decide to delimit the number of countries within their analysis. It is for this reason that the majority of studies within comparative sport policy/ management literature tend to favour small-N studies with the selection of a handful of countries based upon predetermined criteria. Comparative researchers are also more likely draw upon and utilise their professional networks to be able to collect the (often large) amounts of data required to make comparisons between nations.

The most common issue relating to the selection of countries is selection bias (Ebbinghaus, 2005; Geddes, 1990; Hug, 2003; Landman & Carvalho, 2017) predicated on preconceived notions of the outcomes that may be exhibited by certain nations. In other words, researchers may select countries on the basis that the country is assumed to exhibit desired outcome(s) (Geddes, 1990). Importantly, such bias can lead to false inferences. It can be argued that the selection of countries based upon the dependent variable is a commonly taken-for-granted convention across many disciplines (Geddes, 1990). Despite this, there is the inherent danger that researchers falsely infer that the similarity between cases is the cause and/or the relationship identified within the sample cases is reflective of the entire population of cases (Geddes, 1990). Both of these issues are problematic for comparative researchers and will likely result in false inferences, miscomparisons or indeterminant findings.

As highlighted previously, it is important to recognise that issues surrounding selection bias affect both large-N studies and small-N studies (Ebbinghaus, 2005; Landman & Carvalho, 2017; Lijphart, 1971). However, Landman and Carvalho (2017) argue that selection bias is less likely to be an issue for large-N studies as they attempt to adhere to the principle of randomisation, despite the commonplace convention within political science that countries are often pre-selected based upon being instances of the dependent variable (Geddes, 1990; Hug, 2003). In contrast, Ebbinghaus (2005) suggests that both small-N and large-N type studies are susceptible to what he describes as the 'problem of contingency', the potential for cases to be pre-selected based upon historical and social processes. For Ebbinghaus (2005), "all comparative research of social entities...faces the same problem of contingency, the fact that the observable pool of macro-social units [i.e., nations] has been shaped by historical social processes" (p. 134). He argues that the complex social and historical process of nation-state formation and international co-operation results in the over- and under-representation of particular types of countries within comparative analysis. The consequence of this pre-determined selection bias of countries is the *"illusion of random sampling"* (p. 135) in that comparative researchers, particularly in large-N studies, assumes that they have a randomised sample when in reality they have a stratified sample, i.e., a sample selected based on some pre-determined criteria (Ebbinghaus, 2005). Issues surrounding selection bias may, in turn, lead to *spuriousness* or *'omitted variable bias'*, the omission of key variables that may account for both the outcome and other explanatory factors already identified. An example of potential spuriousness is evident within De Bosscher et al.'s (2006) theoretical framework of the sport policies factors that explain international sporting success. This framework identified nine policy areas (or variables) which impacted the outcome of elite sport success (absolute medal count). In their model, they also included an additional tenth policy area, i.e., the recognition of the role of the media, although this was never fully analysed. Nonetheless, its very inclusion within the original SPLISS framework acknowledges that this is a potentially confounding variable that may or may not influence elite sport success. Landman and Carvalho (2017) suggest that the only potential strategy for mitigating the issue of spuriousness is for researchers to specify all potentially relevant variables that may account for the observed outcome or make a deliberate selection of countries and, in doing so, recognise the limitations and trade-offs of this approach.

PROTOCOL STANDARDISATION

A fourth practical issue is the need to ensure consistency across the social units compared. On the assumption that researchers or countries have been selected based on making comparisons, given the significant political, social and cultural differences that exist between different countries (all of which come with their own assumptions, experiences, expectations and norms), there is a need for comparative researchers to ensure consistency regarding their data collection and analysis. In other words, comparative researchers need to ensure that their protocols and procedures are standardised across all social units compared. As Jowell (1998) notes, "rules about sample coverage, sampling method, calculation of response rates, fieldwork periods, and so on should be clear, unambiguous, and capable of being implemented with more or less equal rigour in all the countries involved" (p. 175). As indicated in Chapter 5 (ensuring equivalence), this does not necessarily mean that all concepts and instruments should be identical as it may be necessary and/or appropriate to adjust them to ensure conceptual and functional equivalence. Nonetheless, all comparative researchers must ensure at least a degree of standardisation across nations so that meaningful comparisons can be made.

One way in which this can be achieved is the development of clear and detailed modus operandi to standardise the data collection and analysis process. In SPLISS 1.0 (De Bosscher et al., 2006) and SPLISS 2.0 (De Bosscher et al., 2015), the research team developed comprehensive modus operandi which specified protocols and sampling procedures but also outlined key stakeholders, defined key concepts and likely data sources. Similarly, Houlihan and Green (2008) and Bergsgard et al. (2007) provided a detailed analytical and conceptual framework by which comparisons could be drawn between nations. In particular, they specified the policy domains in which key informants/researchers should focus their analysis whilst allowing a degree of freedom and flexibility to enable local researchers to discuss features which may be unique to particular sporting contexts. In all these studies, the researchers have deployed standardised procedures to enable comparisons to be made. The balancing act for the comparative researcher is to ensure sufficient rigorous and standardised protocols are in place, whilst at the same time having a degree of flexibility to avoid infringing upon socio-cultural norms and capturing the differences between nations. One potential strategy that can be employed to ensure both standardisation and flexibility is to develop instruments and protocols through collaboration with participating nations (vis-à-vis researchers). In practice, however, adopting a collaborative approach to developing instruments and protocols is much easier said than done, and the decision to adopt this approach will likely result in a number of additional logistical and practical issues, especially as more countries are included within the sample (Jowell, 1998).

DATA TIME-LAG

Another practical issue faced by comparative researchers is the time-lag or amount of time between collecting and analysing data and publishing results. The difference between data collection and publication can commonly range between two to four years. Within the comparative elite sport policy/management literature, it is common for there to be a sizable amount of time between data collection and publication. The interview data collected as part of Green and Houlihan's (2005) analysis of policy change and prioritisation of elite sport across the United Kingdom, Canada and Australia, for example, were collected as part of Mick Green's doctoral thesis between February and October 2002 and subsequently published in January 2003 (Green, 2003). Therefore, the empirical data utilised for their analysis were collected at least 3 years before being published. Similarly, part of the data collected for Bergsgard et al.'s (2007) analysis of elite sport systems was collected 3 years before publication (2004 onwards).

127

This sort of time-period between data collection and publication of results is not uncommon across many scientific disciplines, but is fairly typical in social and political sciences due to the time taken to produce outputs such as journal articles and books, etc. The time-lag from the point of data collection to publication (i.e., 2 to 4 years within the comparative sport policy domain) can render comparative data at best, historical, or at worst, outdated and meaningless. Furthermore, given that national political cycles are not synchronised with each other, or to the cycles of elite sport for that matter, there is a danger of misalignment with data that may be accurate on the day of collection but do not represent the current political reality (Jowell, 1998). This is not to mention the further compounding issue of potential exogenous shocks to either sporting or political systems such as unforeseeable changes in government policy and funding, or uncontrollable events such as a crash in stock markets, economic recessions or global pandemics. Quite to what extent there is a solution to this issue beyond the obvious attempts to either speed up the research process or shorten the data collection period is debatable. It is more likely that comparative researchers should at least acknowledge this limitation when presenting their findings and in doing so recognise that the findings presented represent comparisons made at a particular period in time.

CROSS-SECTIONAL DATA LIMITATIONS

Not only does the time-lag issue make comparisons limited and outdated, but it also makes comparisons between two different time periods quite problematic. Is it fair and/ or accurate, for example, to compare the development of elite sport systems from the early 1990s to present given the significant social, political and economic differences and characteristics between these time-periods? This is perhaps why, amongst other reasons, the SPLISS consortium has been careful in not drawing too many comparisons between SPLISS 1.0 (De Bosscher et al., 2006) and SPLISS 2.0 (De Bosscher et al., 2015). The limitations associated with cross-sectional analysis are important as, "comparative studies generally produce a time-bound analysis and thus take no account of the differential rate at which issues might emerge and mature, nor of the variation in the period over which policy is determined and implemented" (Houlihan, 1997, p. 11). Comparative studies, therefore, typically only provide a 'snapshot' of a particular phenomenon, rather than considering how it developed or evolved. De Bosscher et al. (2015) referred to this limitation as the 'instant picture' (p. 80), whereby the comparative study examines elite sport statically (i.e., at a single point in time), while recognising that elite sport development is dynamic and constantly evolving. This is not to suggest that this approach is not useful or valid, but rather that most comparative studies are not time-bound and therefore do not give a sense of how the phenomena have changed over time. It is important for comparative research to explicitly recognise this particular limitation as it will help us recognise the value of, and need for more, longitudinal comparative studies that examine how phenomena change over time. Such studies would help policy-makers, practitioners and researchers to better understand the nature and scope of change that is occurring within and across sport organisations and systems.

FUNDING AND RESOURCE CONSTRAINTS

A final practical issue for data collection and analysis relates to the funding and resource constraints that are imposed upon comparative studies. The practical reality is that comparative research is often a costly endeavour requiring significant funding to support planning and implementation efforts. Comparative researchers are often dependent upon external funding sources to carry out their studies, for example through national research councils, governmental sporting or sport-related agencies. In discussing the potential limitations of this dependency, Øyen (1990) suggests that many of the stakeholders that have a vested (likely financial) interest in comparative studies will often give preferential treatment to their own country and seek scientific or even pseudo-scientific evidence to support their political agendas. This is rather ironic given that some comparative scholars have suggested that the general purpose of carrying out comparative research is to avoid ethnocentrism (Dogan & Pelassy, 1990). Thus, whilst comparative analysis may have the potential benefit of enabling us to learn from different countries, it nonetheless can be used by policy- and decision-makers for more pragmatic or political purposes.

The consequence of this dependency is that researchers may be restricted by the requirements or conditions of their funders. This can manifest in several ways, but in particular, it can lead comparative researchers to design and execute studies in such a manner as to appease their funders. In some instances, this can be multiple-funding partners such as governmental organisations or agencies, all of whom may have different requirements, focuses and purposes. In this instance, the comparative researcher(s) is required to balance these expectations and interests to satisfy all their funding partners. In addition, issues surrounding funding and resources constraints can also lead to differences in the approaches adopted in terms of data output and presentation. Much in the same way consultants might be tempted to present their findings in such a manner as to appease or satisfy their client, comparative researchers should be cognisant of how their studies have been informed and influenced by their external funding bodies. Furthermore, how comparative data are presented can be heavily influenced by these external funding agencies. It is to these issues regarding data output and presentation to which we now turn.

DATA OUTPUT – PRESENTATION AND GENERALISATION

This next set of practical issues relates to how comparative data and study findings are presented by researchers and how the findings of comparative studies are utilised by decision/policy-makers to inform their strategic planning and processes (Hantrais, 2009; Landman & Carvalho, 2017; Øyen, 1990; Schuster, 2007). Once the data have been collected, it is the task of a comparative researcher to logically organise and manage (often large) amounts of data (often in various forms) in such a manner to respond to the research question or hypothesis statement(s); or more practically speaking, to make some sense of the data so that they can be presented to decision- and policy-makers. Far from an easy and straightforward afterthought of the research process, several practical issues can occur when attempting to present comparative data and comparative study findings. These issues include, but are not limited to: data reduction/oversimplification, overstatement of study findings, indeterminant study findings and misinterpretation of generalisability.

DATA REDUCTION/OVERSIMPLIFICATION

Data output issues, and how comparative data should be disseminated, depend to a large extent upon the original purpose of the study and how studies are funded (Landman & Carvalho, 2017). If a study is seeking to produce highly descriptive accounts of a sporting nation, then it is likely that the data will be presented as such. If the data are being used to test causal relationships between variables, then they are likely to be presented very differently. This difference between approaches to data presentation is evident within the comparative sport policy/management literature with some scholars choosing to present their findings as radar graphs and traffic lights derived from a scoring system of critical success factors and others choosing to present their findings as general statements (cf. De Bosscher et al., 2009, 2015 vs. Andersen & Ronglan, 2012; Bergsgard et al., 2007; Green & Houlihan, 2005)

The temptation when managing such large datasets may be to reduce and simplify findings to make them more manageable and presentable. It is recognised that data reduction is an important and necessary part of the research process, but there is an inherent danger in reducing highly rich, detailed and culturally-laden data to a single (or multiple) table, graphs or traffic light systems. While tables and graphs may be aesthetically pleasing and/or even politically attractive, they often serve a limited explanatory purpose. An example would be if you were to scale a country based on the degree to which they have an advanced talent identification and development programme. Inevitably, this requires the researchers to develop an arbitrary scoring system for each variable compared and often make (likely a qualitative) judgement on whether an entire nation scores a '4' or a '5' based on the empirical evidence collected. While it might be tempting to compare scores across nations by piloting their progress on a radar graph to see how one sporting nation compares to another or the entire sample, we argue this has little analytical value. What does it mean to score '3' out of a possible '5' on this scale?

Issues relating to data reduction and oversimplification are particularly evident within large-N, variable-oriented comparative studies as they adhere to a reductionist logic (Creswell & Creswell, 2018; Ragin, 2014). It should be noted, however, that these issues are also evident in case-oriented comparative studies, especially when attempting to develop an accessible narrative surrounding the empirical data collected. Data reduction is a constant challenge for social scientists and is of particular concern for comparative researchers primarily due to the large amount of data often collected for comparative studies. Thus, it is important that comparative researchers are mindful of the challenge and careful not to reduce data in such a manner as to lose its richness and meaning. Ultimately, this issue can be seen to represent a clear trade-off between accessibility and simplicity to get across the findings of a comparative study, on the one hand, versus accuracy and capturing the complexity of social reality on the other.

OVERSTATING STUDY FINDINGS

The methodological limitations and practical issues detailed in this chapter highlight why it is important for comparative sport researchers not to overstate their research findings. Not only are there a series of methodological and practical trade-offs that must be made when attempting to compare sporting nations, but the issues of selection bias and spuriousness in particular suggest that there could be many other confounding variables that may or may not explain the outcomes observed. By its very nature, comparative research occurs within a 'real-world' setting and therefore it is not possible to control for all possible variables which may explain a particular outcome (Lijphart, 1971). It is often not possible to draw firm conclusions unless the study includes the entire sample population so that a researcher has complete information to be able to confirm or refute a hypothesis (Geddes, 1990). Even with the most comprehensive datasets, comparative researchers must be cautious about making inferences and should be careful in ensuring that they are as enthusiastic about their limitations as they are about their research findings (Jowell, 1998).

Overstating findings can also lead to a more fundamental practical issue relating to how findings are utilised by policy- and decision-makers to inform their strategic planning and processes. If comparative researchers make false inferences or 'miscompare' (Sartori, 1994), then there is an inherent danger that policy- or decision-makers will also be making potentially misinformed decisions based upon either indeterminant (see below) or inaccurate research findings. It is in this sense that comparative researchers (and all social scientists for that matter) have an ethical responsibility and a moral duty to ensure the accuracy of their findings and acknowledge the limitations of their approaches so that they are neither misunderstood nor overstated by others.

Related to the previously mentioned issue of data sensitivity, the extent to which individual countries that participate in research may also benefit from their inclusion may be important to acknowledge. Schuster (2007) cautions that

> ...both independent analysts and government agencies find it difficult to resist the temptation of comparing the participation rates in their country to several other (often carefully) selected countries, and the cultural policy literature is now littered with such comparisons. But too often this temptation has led to reducing the available data to perfunctory comparisons intended to demonstrate one assertion or another or, worse, to constructing crude league tables that are, at the very least, misleading (p. 100).

It is important, therefore, to consider how such comparative research will be used for political purposes that fit specific policy agendas or political arguments, rather than an overall public good (Schuster, 2007).

INDETERMINANT STUDY FINDINGS

Closely linked to the issue of overstating study findings is the potential pitfall of indeterminant study findings. An indeterminant study within comparative analysis refers to a study that is "designed in such a way that the research question cannot truly be answered" (Landman & Carvalho, 2017, p. 306). The most common explanation for indeterminant study findings is the identification of more variables for a particular outcome where there are not enough countries in which to be able to determine the key explanatory factors, hence the results cannot be determined. It is for this reason that indeterminant study findings are also closely related to data access/recruitment and the "too many variables, not enough cases problem" (see Chapter 4 – sampling), although it is often not apparent that a study might be indeterminant until the data analysis/output stage, as it is not possible to identify or predict the potential number of explanatory variables.

Despite the issue often only being realised or evident at the later stage of the research process, many potential strategies can be employed to avoid this particularly non-desirable outcome. Lijphart (1971) identified three potential strategies in attempting to avoid this issue. These include (i) increasing the number of cases within the research design to enable the researcher to identify the key explanatory factors; although in practice this is often not possible or practically feasible. The researcher might also be able to (ii) combine variables to reduce the overall number of variables, but this would not necessarily ensure that an indeterminant study outcome would not occur. Another strategy is to (iii) only focus on comparable cases which would help to avoid the problem, but may reduce the sample of social entities studied (Lijphart, 1971).

MISINTERPRETATION OF GENERALISABILITY

The above issues of overstating findings and the potential pitfall of indeterminant study findings are further complicated when findings from one country can be generalised to another. As discussed in Chapter 3 (why compare), comparative researchers attempt to make inferences and generalisations in order to make comparisons. These inferences are fundamental to the comparative process in that they involve "an attempt to infer beyond the immediate data to something broader that is not directly observed" (Della Porta, 2008, p. 199). The concept of generalisability and how comparative researchers make inferences based upon the data is often misunderstood by academics and practitioners alike; this is evident within case-oriented research in general (Flyvbjerg, 2006) and within the context of sport specifically (Smith, 2018).

There are two issues regarding generalisability that are of particular concern for those seeking to make comparisons. The first considers the extent to which it is possible to transpose general learnings from one country to another. Houlihan (1997) argues in his comparative sport policy analysis of five countries that comparative sport scholars should be sensitive "to the dangers of transposing the policy experience of one country to another uncritically and without qualification" (p. 4). He goes on to argue that yet another issue of comparative analysis "concerns the misinterpretation of results and the temptation to build elaborate analysis on the basis of weak or limited data" (p. 5). This issue can manifest itself in more specific elements of elite sport systems, such as talent ID and development programmes. In discussing the transposition of ideas and programmes from the former Soviet Union and Eastern Blocs, Collins and Bailey (2012) forewarn of the sciences of countries adopting second-hand talent ID and development frameworks that are simply copied and pasted from one policy context to another.

The second issue is the extent to which it is possible to generalise or make inferences from the findings of a comparative study beyond the selected sample. As a consequence of the abovementioned data collection and analysis issues, many comparative researchers are deliberately tentative and cautious about drawing broader inferences regarding the extent to which their findings beyond their sample apply to, or can be useful for, the broader population. Despite this, it is easy to see how academics or practitioners alike might be tempted to draw broader inferences about the study findings to countries beyond the initial data set. This is especially the case for those who are neither familiar with the methodology employed nor the limitations of the comparative approach. Academics and practitioners should resist this temptation and be cautious about making inferences and generalisations beyond the selected sample and fully acknowledge the limitations of the study.

CHAPTER SUMMARY

This chapter has summarised the practical issues faced by comparative researchers when collecting and analysing data. The practical issues identified herein are not exhaustive, but the chapter does serve to indicate the nature and extent of the challenge that lies ahead for those seeking to make comparisons. The chapter has also identified some potential strategies that can be used by comparative researchers to overcome (or at least mitigate) data collection, analysis and output-related issues. What can be drawn from this discussion is that in some cases it is simply not possible to mitigate the practical issues either because they more accurately represent some sort of trade-off or compromise or because these issues are an inevitable outcome of conducting comparative analysis. Nonetheless, it is hoped that the strategies identified herein help comparative researchers to conduct and share transparent and accurate research findings. To reiterate, it is only once comparative researchers develop more conscious thinking in their comparative analysis and openly acknowledge and embrace the likely pitfalls, methodological trade-offs and practical challenges will they be able to navigate these issues more effectively.

PART III

DECONSTRUCTING COMPARATIVE ANALYSIS — COMMON THEMES AND NEW DIRECTIONS

CHAPTER 7

Comparative Analysis Within Sport: Challenging the Orthodoxy and Avoiding the Doldrums

Chapter objectives

- To review the aims/objectives of the book and how these have been achieved;
- To reiterate the shortcomings of the comparative sport literature and outline the contribution of the book to the comparative inquiry in sport;
- To discuss how comparative research within sport can be advanced.

This book has outlined the theory and method of how to compare sporting nations, and in doing so offers a modest but important contribution to the comparative sport literature by explicitly articulating the logic of comparative inquiry in sport. The book has focused on the fundamental issues of comparative analysis in sport including *why* we seek to make comparisons along with the philosophical assumptions and knowledge claims (Chapter 2) and varying motivations and theoretical perspectives (Chapter 3) that underpin it. In addition, it has addressed issues regarding *how* it may be possible to compare sporting nations including how to select countries (Chapter 4), how to ensure equivalence of apparatus and procedures employed, (Chapter 5) and how to deal with specific practical issues faced by a comparative researcher when seeking to compare sporting nations (Chapter 6). What, then, can be drawn more broadly from this explicit discussion of the theory and method of comparative analysis in sport, and how might this help to advance or, at least, inform future studies that seek to compare sporting nations?

There are a number of specific themes that can be drawn from the previous chapters which offer some potential insights into how comparative research within sport more broadly, and comparative analysis within elite sport policy/management in particular, can be enhanced. The first theme threaded throughout the discussion is the importance of explicitly recognising the methodological trade-offs, challenges and limitations of comparative analysis within sport. Simply put, it is not easy to make meaningful comparisons of sporting nations and there are no shortcuts or quick fixes for many of the challenges and issues that comparative researchers might face. What can also be drawn from the discussion of sample selection (Chapter 4), issues of equivalence (Chapter 5), and the practical issues of conducting comparative analysis in sport (Chapter 6) is that many of the issues faced by comparative sport researchers inevitably involve having to make a number of compromises or methodological trade-offs in order to compare sporting nations. These decisions often depend upon the motivations that drive and underpin the study and the particular outcomes that are sought (Chapter 3). The choices that researchers make with regards to their comparative methodological design are not impartial, and the decisions taken are seldom neutral or immutable. Like objects of inquiry, they are socially, and not infrequently politically, constructed. Comparative research designs are drawn up and implemented by human beings with their own personalities, cultures, ideologies and agendas (Hantrais, 2009, p. 70). It is perhaps for this reason that the comparative method can best be understood as an, 'art rather than a science' and why comparative analysis is described as imperfect (Lijphart, 1971; Øyen, 1990).

For these reasons, we are empathic to those who are seek to make comparisons between sporting nations. The work is challenging, yet important in advancing our collective insights into sport and society. This book has sought to help in this endeavour by outlining a philosophical and methodological framework for comparing sporting nations (Chapter 2) and discussing the various components within it. In this way it is a useful primer for anyone seeking to make comparisons for the first time or perhaps wanting to be able to adequately assess the findings of other comparative studies. In being able to recognise and articulate the philosophical assumptions, methodological challenges and practical limitations that are part and parcel of the comparative research process, researchers will be better equipped to design and execute clear and well-reasoned studies that openly discuss limitations and how these limitations influence the nature and extent of the findings sought.

The second general theme, which has been implicitly argued throughout the book, is that the *comparativists'* viewpoint (Øyen, 1990) is the most appropriate when seeking to compare sporting nations. We believe that the advancement of comparative research in sport can only occur through further questioning of the distinctive characteristics of comparative analysis. For this reason, it is important for all those attempting to make meaningful comparisons between sporting nations should develop a deeper understanding of, and appreciation for, comparative methods. The outcome of focusing more explicitly on the theory and method of comparative analysis within sport is the generation of what Sartori (1970) referred to as a more 'conscious thinkers', i.e., comparative social scientists that are more acutely aware of the theory and method of comparative analysis along with all its potential challenges, pitfalls, trade-offs and limitations. It is in this tradition that we have sought to embrace *'comparativist'* thinking and make explicit – and to a large extent more accessible – what some comparative sport scholars have often assumed to be understood by both researchers and practitioners alike, namely the logic of comparative inquiry and the methodological and practical challenges and limitations that are faced when attempting to compare sporting nations.

In this regard, all comparative sport researchers should be reminded of Jowell's remarks about being as enthusiastic about their methodological and practical limitations as they are their explanatory findings (Jowell, 1998). It is only once comparative researchers fully embrace comparative methodology, along with its challenges, limitations, compromises, and trade-offs, that it will it be possible to move from *ignorants* (i.e., those who choose to overlook or ignore the issues of comparative inquiry) to *comparativists* (who understand and embrace the theoretical and methodological challenges and difficulties of comparative inquiry) and thus advance comparative research in sport. Ultimately, this requires a shift in thinking (or at least emphasis) for those who are currently undertaking or are intending to conduct comparative analysis within sport. This shift requires researchers to recognise and embrace comparative methodology rather than view it as a (un)necessary hurdle that needs to be overcome order to make interesting comparisons between sporting nations.

ADVANCING COMPARATIVE SPORT RESEARCH

In addition to the general themes detailed above, there are a number of specific themes to draw from the discussion of the theory and method of comparative inquiry in sport. These themes relate to the elite sport policy/management domain in particular, but also have applicability to, and have relevance for, many other sub-disciplines within sport.

The first theme emphasises the need to explicitly incorporate and adopt strategies that can be used to overcome or at least mitigate the challenges and limitations of comparative inquiry. This book has offered many practical examples of ways in which comparative researchers can mitigate the potential issues faced when conducting comparative research – many of which have not been explicitly utilised or adopted by comparative researchers within the elite sport policy/management domain. As has been argued throughout this book, it is important to acknowledge that these strategies do not offer a magic wand to solve all problems faced by comparative sport researchers, but rather they should help appropriately manage and mitigate challenges, and control for potentially confounding variables. Seen from this viewpoint, even the most well-conceived and planned for comparative sport study will to some extent be defeated by its own taxonomy and technique (Øyen, 1990). However, by adopting a comparativist viewpoint, and in becoming more conscious thinkers, we might be able to more effectively challenge those who criticise comparative analysis in sport as being too general, not methodologically rigorous, or not of any particular value.

A second theme that can be drawn from assessing the comparative elite sport policy/management domain is the need for greater plurality of philosophical traditions and methods utilised by comparative sport researchers. The majority of studies within the elite sport policy/management domain adopt either a *positivist* or *post-positivist* philosophical viewpoint when comparing sporting nations. This is not necessarily an issue in and of itself and it should be re-stated that these studies have provided valuable insights into the similarities and differences that may or may not exist between elite sport development systems. Nonetheless, as noted within the discussion of assumptions that underpin comparative research (Chapter 2), it is important to recognise that many of these studies are informed by the same philosophical assumptions. Consequently, they are likely to offer the same types of knowledge claims regarding the similarities and differences that exist between sporting nations. Thus, we would suggest that there is a need for a greater plurality of both philosophical and methodological approaches, not just for the sake of plurality, but rather to generate new and innovative ways to make comparisons between sporting nations and to ultimately produce alternative ways with which we can understand our social world.

A third theme which can be drawn from the discussions of philosophical assumptions and knowledge claims (Chapter 2), the motivations for comparing sporting nations (Chapter 3), and sample selection (Chapter 4) is the importance of recognising the limitations and assumptions of both large-N, nomothetic, variable-oriented type studies on the one hand and small-N, ideographic, case-study oriented, comparative studies on the other. The former type of studies (large-N/nomothetic/variable-oriented) have traditionally dominated comparative inquiry (Lijphart, 1971) and it appears this dominance is also reflected within the contemporary elite sport management/policy domain. Consistent with several other comparative scholars (e.g., Dogan & Pelassy, 1990; Landman & Carvalho, 2017; Ragin, 2006, 2014; Rihoux & Ragin, 2012), we suggest that both of these general approaches have merit and can be used to compare sporting nations. It is equally important to recognise that they both have their relative weaknesses, which should be acknowledged when conducting any comparative study. Our discussion of the elite sport policy/management domain indicates that there appears to be imbalance in these approaches. First, there are many small-N, case-based studies which have been single-country studies that have produced largely *descriptive* rather than *predictive* accounts of sporting nations (Landman & Carvalho, 2017). Whilst single-country comparative studies are valuable, it is important to recognise the limitations of these studies, which have limited generalisability beyond their sample population, and limited potential to identify the causal factors that explain the similarities and differences between nations (Lijphart, 1971). Ultimately, if sport scholars wish to identify the underlying causal or generative mechanisms that explain elite sport success, there is a need to move beyond descriptive and single-based studies towards more hypothesis- and predictive-driven analysis (Landman & Carvalho, 2017). A good example of how this can be achieved from a single-case study is De Bosscher et al. (2011) which examined the effectiveness of national elite sport policies through a single-case study of Flanders. The purpose of the study was primarily to develop a framework to assess effectiveness of elite sport policies of nations across all nations.

This is not to suggest that there is a need to focus exclusively on more large-N type comparative studies. While such studies can offer valuable insights, they also encompass problematic limitations and assumptions. Large-N type, variable-oriented studies, despite their infrequency within the elite sport policy/management field, have become dominant and therefore increasingly well-known, without much in the way of criticism or challenge. This situation led Henry et al. (2020) to suggest that variable-oriented research has become the new orthodoxy in comparative sport policy research (see the case study at the end of this chapter). In short, the philosophical differences between approaches to comparing sporting nations has divided the comparative sport field between those who favour the large-N, nomothetic, variable-oriented approaches, and those who prefer small-N, ideographic, case-based approaches.

Moving forward then, perhaps a fruitful avenue for comparative researchers could be to explore the potential to cross these divides, at least as much as is ontologically and epistemologically possible. Some studies within the elite sport policy/management domain have recently attempted to do this. De Bosscher (2018), for example, puts forward what they describe as a mixed-methods approach for comparing sporting nations, although the extent to which their analysis represents a genuine mixed-methods approach remains open to debate (Henry et al., 2020). Nonetheless, De Bosscher and colleagues' recent attempts demonstrate the potential utility of combining both qualitative and quantitative approaches in developing accounts of sporting nations. Other approaches that have yet to be fully embraced by sport scholars are more configurational, such as the qualitative case analysis (QCA) or fuzzy-set analysis (Ragin, 2014; Rihoux & Ragin, 2012). These methods attempt to combine different sampling strategies and variable-oriented and case-based approaches to produce more nuanced and holistic understandings of the similarities and differences between countries than what is permitted by traditional methods. Equally, what can be drawn from the specific discussions of sampling procedures is the potential benefits of moving beyond the simple dichotomies and the MSSD/MDSD divide to adopt alternative sampling approaches/designs (e.g., MSDO and MSSO). Wagner and Hanstad's (2011) comparative analysis of anti-doping regulations within Scandinavian countries is an example of how an alternative sampling strategy, the Most Different Similar Outcome/Most Similar Different Outcome (MDSO/MSDO) strategies can be employed to understand the similarities and differences in responses to broader institutional changes by sporting nations.

Our fourth specific theme relates to the overall trajectory of the comparative elite sport policy/management literature, which has become increasingly dominated by specific conceptual and methodological research templates, particularly variable-oriented templates. Such pragmatism encourages researchers to conduct comparative studies in a particular way, using either the same (or similar) conceptual and methodological approaches without consideration of the alternatives. The inherent danger here is that comparative sport scholarship runs the risk of becoming *'template-driven'* research and being lured into *the doldrums* of how comparative inquiry in sport *ought* to or *should* be done. More generally, in the social sciences, Ragin (2006) warns that the outcome of template-driven research is that "researchers view their primary task as one of assessing the relative importance of causal variables drawn from competing theories...in practice, however, most theories in the social sciences are vague when it comes to specifying both causal conditions and outcomes" (p. 634). Ragin (2006) goes on to suggest that there are two related outcomes of template-driven research: the continued production of general lists of potentially relevant causal variables and the generation of weak theory.

If comparative sport researchers were to be lured into the doldrums of template-driven research within sport, there is a potential for them to only see comparative sport scholarship through a particular conceptual, theoretical or methodological lens. These conceptual, theoretical or methodological approaches then become the established orthodoxy, leaving little room for alternative, perhaps more fruitful, ways to compare sporting nations. A critical reading of the progress of comparative sport policy/ management scholarship to date could be that it has only been able to produce general characterisations of social phenomena without being able to sufficiently address its causal complexity. In other words, it has yet to be able to specify the explanatory factors which lead to elite sport success – at least with any degree of certainty. A counter argument to this critical viewpoint might be that these general characterisations of sporting nations are, in part, due to the nature of the unit of analysis employed within comparative inquiry, which often requires researchers to make broad sweeping inferences and generalisations regarding the structures and processes across nations. Perhaps yet another explanation could be that the field of comparative elite sport policy/management still remains in its infancy with much more to offer in terms of generating theories about elite international sport and the similarities and differences between sporting nations.

A fifth theme relates to the application of comparative methodology across various sub-disciplines within the sport policy/management literature. Although this book has focused predominantly on the elite sport development literature, with only a few exceptions, the comparative tradition has yet to establish itself in the same way within other sub-research areas across the sport policy/management domain. The limited application of comparative methodology within other sub-research domains may, in part, be explained by the relative imbalance of certain philosophical positions and variable-oriented research in general, which has led to the aforementioned issues relating to assumptions around how or in what ways comparative research ought to be done and by whom. There are, however, many sub-research domains whereby the comparative methodological approach might be particularly applicable and/or useful if fully embraced by researchers. These include, but are not are not limited to, the study of mega-events and legacies, sport governance and leadership, international relations and diplomacy, marketing and sponsorship, and strategic management and organisational change. These particular research domains might benefit further from a macro-environmental analysis between countries (or at least larger social units) insofar as it could help to identify similarities and differences, and how policy and practice may continue to be advanced over future years. Addressing the aforementioned imbalances and articulating more clearly and explicitly the logic of comparative inquiry in sport is perhaps a starting point and may go some way to encouraging more sport scholars to adopt comparative methodological approaches within their research.

CASE STUDY 6: CHALLENGING THE ORTHODOXY OF VARIABLE-ORIENTED APPROACHES TO COMPARING SPORTING NATIONS (HENRY ET AL., 2020)

Henry et al. (2020) provide a rare example of an attempt to challenge variable-oriented approaches to comparing sporting nations. In particular, their analysis focuses on the 'SPLISS' framework proposed by De Bosscher and colleagues. This framework identifies 9 policy areas (or 'pillars'), comprised of 105 critical success factors (CSFs) that lead to international sport success. In utilising this framework, De Bosscher and colleagues (also known as the SPLISS consortium) then pilot tested the application of the framework with the aim of benchmarking the sport policy factors leading to international sporting success in six countries: Belgium (Flanders and Wallonia), Canada, Italy, the Netherlands, Norway and the United Kingdom (De Bosscher et al., 2010; De Bosscher et al., 2006, 2009). De Bosscher and colleagues then carried out a larger follow up study, SPLISS 2.0 (De Bosscher et al., 2015), which sought to better understand which (and how) sport policies lead to international sporting success in 13 nations and 3 regions. These included: Belgium (Wallonia and Flanders), Canada, the Netherlands, Denmark, Estonia, Finland, France, Northern Ireland, Portugal, Spain, Switzerland, South Korea, Japan, Australia and Brazil).

According to Henry et al. (2020), what is unique about the SPLISS account of elite sport systems is its emphasis on causal relationships through the adoption of a logic model (input-throughput-output) approach to explain elite sport success – see the table below. In both the SPLISS 1.0 and SPLISS 2.0 studies, the researchers adopt a variable-oriented approach to assess the similarities and differences between sporting nations. The difference between the SPLISS 1.0 and 2.0 studies is that the former adopts a more explicit positivist approach compared to the 2.0 version.

SPLISS's variable-oriented 'input-throughout-input' account of elite sport success

Inputs	Throughputs	Outputs
Financial and human resources	Integrated approach to policy development	Medals won (absolute or relative)
Funding (NGBs)	Foundation and participation	Market share (%)
	Talent ID and development	
	Athletic and post-career support	
	Training facilities	
	Coaching provision and coach development	
	(Inter)national competition	
	Scientific research	

Adapted from: De Bosscher et al. (2006)

In their article, Henry and colleagues (Henry et al., 2020) provide a historical overview of the elite sport policy/management literature, focusing on the advancements of making international comparisons between elite sport systems and how the SPLISS account has emerged as what they describe as an increasingly orthodox and variable-oriented account of elite sport policy. Furthermore, the authors argue that *"the hegemony of the SPLISS approach in the field of analysis of the factors critical to elite sport policy success has been very evident in the mobilization of an active 'industry' of SPLISS papers and associated conferences and workshops"* (p. 14). In challenging this orthodoxy and the variable-oriented approach in general, Henry and colleagues outline six critiques of the SPLISS account. They include: (i) philosophical assumptions and the identification of causal variables, (ii) the 'black box' problem, (iii) internal validity, (iv) non-equivalence and reliability, (v) overlooking/ignoring agency, and (vi) reductionism and mixed-methods.

(i) Philosophical assumptions and the identification of causal variables – challenges the SPLISS studies on the basis of whether the independent variables identified through the SPLISS framework can claim to be explanatory factors and that a more causal account could be achieved through the adoption of a realist evaluation approach.

(ii) The 'black box' problem – This issue relates to David Easton's (1957) systems model whereby he draws upon the analogy of a black box to explain the policy process. Henry et al. argue that the SPLISS account has yet to resolve the black box problem in that, although you might be able to identify measurable inputs, the processes which turn these inputs into outcomes is not directly observed.

(iii) Internal validity – Henry at al. also challenge the SPLISS account on the basis of its internal validity, i.e., whether outcomes observed in the study (medals won/ market share) were due to changes in an independent variable (pillars/CSFs), and not to some other, external factor(s).

(vi) Non-equivalence and reliability – The authors criticise the SPLISS studies on the basis of their functional and sampling equivalence, the former being issues related to the primary and secondary data collected and the latter with regards to the pragmatic sampling strategy employed by De Bosscher and colleagues, which Henry et al. argue is stratified rather than random.

(v) Overlooking/ignoring agency – Henry et al. argue that it is not possible to separate the meso from the micro and macro level of analysis. They argue that the variable-oriented approach runs the risk of over-emphasising structuralist explanations of elite sport policy, and therefore overlooks/ignores the role of individuals and agency within the process.

(vi) Reductionism and mixed-methods – Challenges the SPLISS account on the basis of its claim to be a mixed-methods approach, taking particular issue with the manner in which the qualitative data are reduced to quantitative measures rather than being subject to qualitative data analytical techniques.

In conclusion, the authors provide an important caveat to their critique of the SPLISS account in that they do *"not seek to deny the contribution to policy explanation and evaluation which variable-based approaches to analysis"* but also emphasise that it is important *"to identify [that] are the limits of such analysis in generating explanations of policy success and the lacunae in such explanations"* (p. 13). In other words, it is not that variable-oriented research is not useful for understanding the similarities and differences that may (or may not) exist between sporting nations, but the limitations should be well developed in order to allow the reader to fully understand what the research shows.

More broadly, Henry and colleagues' analysis of the variable-oriented approach of comparing sporting nations through a critique of the SPLISS account is both symptomatic and reflective of the divide that exists within the sport policy/management literature. This divide relates to those who emphasise large-N, nomothetic, variable-oriented research versus those who emphasise small-N, ideographic, case-based oriented research. The differences in these methodological approaches often stem from more fundamental philosophical disagreements about what constitutes reality (ontology) and how knowledge can be gathered (epistemology) – see Chapter 3 (philosophical assumptions and knowledge claims).

KEY CHAPTER READING – COMPARING SPORTING NATIONS

Introduction: The logic of comparative inquiry in sport	Øyen (1990), Landman and Carvalho (2017)
Chapter 1: Is it possible to compare apples with oranges? The difficulties and challenges of comparing sporting nations	Dowling et al., (2018); Hofstede (1998), Jowell (1998); Landman and Carvalho (2017); Schuster (2007); Øyen (1990)
Chapter 3: Philosophical assumptions and knowledge claims of comparing sporting nations	Ancker, (2008); Creswell and Creswell (2018); Grix (2010); Landman and Carvalho (2017)
Chapter 3: Why compare sporting nations? Purpose, goals and unit of analysis	Dogan and Pélassy (1990); Hantrais (2009) pp. 9-11; Landman and Carvalho (2017)
Chapter 4: Selecting countries (sample)	Ancker (2008); Della Porta (2008). Dogan and Pélassy (1990); Ebbinghaus (2005); Hantrais (2009); Hofstede (1998); Landman and Carvalho (2017); Lijphart (1971); Przeworski and Teune (1982); Teune (1990); Øyen (1990); Lijphart (1971)
Chapter 5: Ensuring construct, sample and functional equivalence	Dogan and Pélassy (1990); Ebbinghaus (2005); Przeworski and Teune (1966); Øyen (1990, 2004); Johnson (1998); Jowell (1998)
Chapter 6: Data collection, analysis and output	Hantrais (2009, pp. 65-71), Houlihan (1997, pp. 3- 13); Landman and Carvalho (2017, pp. 29-95)
Chapter 7: Comparative analysis within sport – Challenging the orthodoxy and avoiding the doldrums	Dowling et al., (2018); Henry et al. (2020); Jowell (1998); Øyen (1990)

KEY CONCEPTS (BY AUTHORS)

Definition Comparative	Øyen (1990) pp. 3-4; Landman and Carvalho (2017); Lijphart (1971)
Comparative method	Della Porta (2008); Landman and Carvalho (2017); Lijphart (1971); Ragin (1987) pp.12-13)
Inferences/logic of comparison	Landman and Carvalho (2017) p. XVII, pp. 14-16; Przeworski and Teune (1970); Ragin (1987) pp. 13-16
Use of theory in comparative inquiry	Dogan and Pélassy (1990) Chapter 4; Landman and Carvalho (2017) Chapter 1; Teune (1990); Creswell and Creswell (2018) Chapter 3 (use of theory); Przeworski and Teune (1970) pp. 17-30, 74-87
Case-based vs. variable-oriented	Ancker (2008); Della Porta (2008); Ragin (1987, 2014); Ragin and Zaret (1983)
Nation state	Dogan and Pélassy (1990); Hantrais (2009) pp.3-4, 51-52; Hofstede (1998); Teune (1990); Øyen (1990)
Large-N vs. small-N	Landman and Carvalho (2017) Chapter 2; Lijphart (1971); Ebbinghaus (2005)
"Too many variables not enough countries/small-N" problem	Ebbinghaus (2005), Landman and Carvalho (2017) pp. 36-39; Lijphart (1971)
Area-based studies	Lijphart (1971), p. 688
MSSD vs. MDSD	Ancker (2008); Della Porta (2008); Landman and Carvalho (2017) Chapter 2; Lijphart (1971); Hantrais (2009) pp. 59-64; Przeworski and Teune (1970); Mills (1850)
Level of analysis (macro, meso, micro)	Landman and Carvalho (2017) pp. 23-25; Ragin (1987) pp. 7-9; Hantrais (2009) pp. 54-56; Przeworski and Teune (1970)
Quantitative vs. qualitative	Creswell and Creswell (2018); Landman and Carvalho (2017) p. 25-26; Grix (2010); Hantrais (2009), p. 65-66; Ragin (1987) pp. 16-18

Equivalence (also see sub-sections below)	Dogan and Pélassy (1990); Ebbinghaus (2005); Johnson (1998); Jowell (1998); Landman and Carvalho (2017); Hantrais (2009), pp. 72-90; Przeworski and Teune (1966), Przeworski and Teune (1970), pp. 91-131; Øyen (1990, 2004); Van Tuyckom et al. (2011)
Construct equivalence	Johnson (1998); Jowell (1998); Hantrais (2009), pp. 73-81; Przeworski and Teune (1966); Øyen (1990, 2004)
Sample equivalence	Øyen (1990, 2004); Ebbinghaus (2005); Hantrais (2009); Jowell (1998); Kohn (1987); Schuster (2007)
Functional equivalence	Davidov et al., 2014; Dogan and Pélassy (1990) Chapter 5 (pp. 37-44), Ebbinghaus (2005); Hantrais (2009); Jowell (1998); Johnson (1998); Mullen (1994); Øyen (1990); Schuster (2007); Stegmueller (2011)
Selection bias	Landman and Carvalho (2017); Ebbinghaus (2005); Geddes (1990); Hug, (2003); King et al. (1994)
Problem of contingency/spuriousness	Landman and Carvalho (2017) pp. 43-50; Ebbinghaus (2005)
Ecological and individualist fallacies	Landman and Carvalho (2017) pp. 50-53
Fruitology	Hofstede (1998); De Bosscher et al. (2006)
QCA/fuzzy sets	Ragin (1987; 2000; 2006; 2014); Rihoux (2006); Rihoux and Ragin (2008)

REFERENCES

Anckar, C. (2008). On the applicability of the most similar systems design and the most different systems design in comparative research. *International Journal of Social Research Methodology*, 11(5), 389–401.

Andersen, S., & Ronglan, L. T. (2012). *Elite Sport: Same Ambitions, Difference Tracks.* Copenhagen Business School.

Baistow, K. (2000). Cross-national research: What can we learn from inter-country comparisons ? *Social Work in Europe*, 7(3), 8–13.

Beacom, A., & Brittain, I. (2016). Public diplomacy and the international paralympic committee: reconciling the roles of disability advocate and sports regulator. *Diplomacy & Statecraft*, 27(2), 273–294. https://doi.org/10.1080/09592296.2016.1169795

Beck, P. J. (2013). 'War minus the shooting': george orwell on international sport and the olympics. *Sport in History*, 33, 72–94.

Berger, P., & Luckman, T. (1966). *The Social Construction of Reality.* Penguin Books.

Bergsgard, N. A., & Norberg, J. R. (2010). Sports policy and politics – the scandinavian way. *Sport in Society*, 13(4), 567-582.

Bergsgard, N., Houlihan, B., Mangset, P., Nodland, S., & Rommetvdet, H. (2007). *Sport Policy: A Comparative Analysis of Stability and Change.* Butterworth-Heinemann.

Bhaskar, R. (1978). *A Realist Theory of Science.* Harvester Press.

Bryman, A. (2015). *Social Research Methods* (5th ed.). Oxford University Press.

Chalip, L., Johnson, A., & Satachura, L. (1996). *National Sports Policies: An International Handbook* (eds.). Greenwood Press.

Collins, D., & Bailey, R. (2012). 'Scienciness' and the allure of second-hand strategy in talent identification and development. *International Journal of Sport Policy and Politics*, 5(2), 1–9. https://doi.org/10.1080/19406940.2012.656682

Creswell, J., & Creswell, D. (2018). *Research design: qualitative, quantitative, and mixed methods approaches* (5th ed.). SAGE Publications.

Crotty, M. (1998). *The foundations of social research: meaning and perspective in the research process.* SAGE Publications.

Darko, N., & Mackintosh, C. (2015). Challenges and constraints in developing and implementing sports policy and provision in Antigua and Barbuda: which way now for a small island state? *International Journal of Sport Policy*, 7(3), 365-390. https://doi.org/10.1080/19406940.2014.925955

Davidov, E., Meuleman, B., Cieciuch, J., Schmidt, P., & Billiet, J. (2014). Measurement equivalence in cross-national research. *Annual Review of Sociology*, 40(1), 55–75.

De Bosscher, V. (2018). A mixed methods approach to compare elite sport policies of nations. A critical reflection on the use of composite indicators in the SPLISS study. *Sport in Society*, 21, 331-355.

De Bosscher, V., De Knop, P., Van Bottenburg, M., & Shibli, S. (2006). A conceptual framework for analysing sports policy factors leading to international sporting success. *European Sport Management Quarterly*, 6(2), 185–215. https://doi.org/10.1080/16184740600955087

De Bosscher, V., De Knop, P., van Bottenburg, M., Shibli, S., & Bingham, J. (2009). Explaining international sporting success: An international comparison of elite sport systems and policies in six countries. *Sport Management Review*, 12(3), 113–136. https://doi.org/10.1016/j.smr.2009.01.001

De Bosscher, V., Heyndels, B., De Knop, P., Van Bottenburg, M., & Shibli, S. (2008). The paradox of measuring success of nations in elite sport. *BELGEO*, 2, 217-234. https://doi.org/10.4000/belgeo.10303

De Bosscher, V., Shibli, S., van Bottenburg, M., de Knop, P., & Truyens, J. (2010). Developing a method for comparing the elite sport systems and policies of nations: A mixed research methods approach. *Journal of Sport Management*, 24(5), 567-600. https://doi.org/10.1123/jsm.24.5.567

De Bosscher, V., Shibli, S., Westerbeek, H., & Van Bottenburg, M. (2015). *Successful Elite Sport Policies: An International Comparison of the Sports Policy Factors Leading to International Sporting Success (SPLISS 2.0) in 15 Nations*. Meyer & Meyer Sport (UK).

De Rycke, J., & De Bosscher, V. (2019). Mapping the potential societal impacts triggered by elite sport: a conceptual framework. *International Journal of Sport Policy and Politics*, 11(3), 485-502. https://doi.org/10.1080/19406940.2019.1581649

Della Porta, D. (2008). *Comparative analysis: case-oriented versus variable-oriented research*. In D. della Porta & M. Keating (Eds.), *Approaches And Methodologies In The Social Sciences: A Pluralist Perspective* (pp. 198–222). Cambridge University Press.

Dennis, M., & Grix, J. (2012). *Sport Under Communism: Behind the East German Miracle*. Palgrave Macmillan UK. https://doi.org/0230227848

Digel, H. (2005). Brief reflections on sport at the beginning of a new century: A German perspective. *Sport in Society*, 8(1). https://doi.org/10.1080/1743043052000316588

Digel, H. (2002). A comparison of competitive sport systems. *New Studies in Athletics*, 17(1), 37–50.

Digel, H. (2005). Comparison of successful sport systems. *New Studies in Athletics*, 20(2), 7–18.

DiMaggio, P, J., & Powell, W. (1983). The iron cage revisited: institutional isomorphism and collective rationality in organizational fields. *American Sociological Review*, 48(2), 147–160.

Dogan, M., & Kazancigil, A. (1994). *Comparing Nations: Concepts, Strategies, Substance*. John Wiley and Sons.

Dogan, M., & Pelassy, D. (1990). *How To Compare Nations: Strategies in Comparative Politics*. Chatham House.

Donnelly, P. (2009). Own the Podium or rent it? Canada's involvement in the global sporting arms race. *Policy Options*, 41–44.

Dowling, M., Brown, P., Legg, D., & Beacom, A. (2018). Living with imperfect comparisons: The challenges and limitations of comparative paralympic sport policy research. *Sport Management Review*, 21(2), 101–113. https://doi.org/10.1016/j.smr.2017.05.002

Dowling, M., Brown, P., Legg, D., & Grix, J. (2018). Deconstructing comparative sport policy analysis: assumptions, challenges, and new directions. *International Journal of Sport Policy and Politics*, 10(4), 687-704. https://doi.org/10.1080/19406940.2018.1530276

Dowling, M., Legg, D., & Brown, P. (2017). *Cross-Comparative Sport Policy Analysis and Paralympic Sport*. In A. Beacom & I. Brittain (Eds.), *Palgrave Handbook of Paralympic Sport*. Palgrave Macmillan UK.

Durkheim, E. (1938). *Rules of Sociological Method*. Chicago University Press.

Easton, D. (1957). *An Approach to the Analysis of Political Systems*. World Politics. https://doi.org/10.2307/2008920

Ebbinghaus, B. (2005). When less is more: selection problems in large-N and small-N cross-national comparisons. *International Sociology*, 20(2), 133–152. https://doi.org/10.1177/0268580905052366

Edwards, A., & Skinner, J. (2009). *Qualitative Research Methods in Sport Management*. Butterworth-Heinemann.

Finer, S. (1971). *Comparative Government*. The Penguin Press.

Flyvbjerg, B. (2006). Five misunderstandings about case-study research. *Qualitative Inquiry*, 12(2), 219-245.https://doi.org/10.1177/1077800405284363

Geddes, B. (1990). How the cases you choose affect the answers you get: Selection bias in comparative politics. *Political Analysis*, 2, 131-150. https://doi.org/10.1093/pan/2.1.131

Geertz, C. (1973). *Thick description: Toward an interpretive theory of culture*. In Interpretation of Cultures. Basic Books.

Green, M. (2003). *An analysis of elite sport policy change in three sports in Canada and the United Kingdom*. Retrieved from: https://hdl.handle.net/2134/7900

Green, M. (2004a). Changing policy priorities for sport in England: The emergence of elite sport development as a key policy concern. *Leisure Studies*, 23(4), 365-385. https://doi.org/10.1080/0261436042000231646

Green, M. (2004b). Power, policy, and political priorities: Elite sport development in Canada and the United Kingdom. *Sociology of Sport Journal*, 21(4), 376-396. https://doi.org/10.1123/ssj.21.4.376

Green, M. (2007). Olympic glory or grassroots development? Sport policy priorities in Australia, Canada and the United Kingdom, 1960-2006. *The International Journal of the History of Sport*, 24(7), 921–953. https://doi.org/10.1080/09523360701311810

Green, M., & Collins, S. (2008). Policy, politics and path dependency: sport development in australia and finland. *Sport Management Review*, 11(3), 225–251. https://doi.org/10.1016/S1441-3523(08)70111-6

Green, M., & Houlihan, B. (2004). Advocacy coalitions and elite sport policy change in canada and the united kingdom. *International Review for the Sociology of Sport*, 39(4), 387-403. https://doi.org/10.1177/1012690204049066

Green, M., & Houlihan, B. (2005). *Elite Sport Development: Policy Learning and Political Priorities*. Routledge.

Green, M., & Houlihan, B. (2006). Governmentality, modernization and the "Disciplining" of national sporting organizations: Athletics in australia and the united kingdom. *Sociology of Sport Journal*, 23(47), 47–71. https://doi.org/10.1123/ssj.23.1.47

Green, M., & Oakley, B. (2001). Elite sport development systems and playing to win: uniformity and diversity in international approaches. *Leisure Studies*, 20, 247–267. https://doi.org/10.1080/02614360110103598

Grix, J. (2010). Introducing "hard" interpretivism and "Q" methodology: Notes from a project on "county sport partnerships and governance." *Leisure Studies*, 29, 457-467. https://doi.org/10.1080/02614367.2010.518290

Grix, J. (2010). *The Foundations of Research* (2nd ed.). Palgrave Macmillan UK.

Grix, J., & Carmichael, F. (2012). Why do governments invest in elite sport? A polemic. *International Journal of Sport Policy and Politics*, 4(1), 73–90. https://doi.org/10.10 80/19406940.2011.627358

Guba, E. G., & Lincoln, Y. S. (1994). *Competing paradigms in qualitative research*. In Y. Lincoln (Eds). *Handbook of qualitative research.* (pp. 105-117). Thousand Oaks.

Hantrais, L. (2009). *International Comparative Research: Theory, Methods and Practice*. Palgrave Macmillan UK.

Harkness, J. (1999). In pursuit of quality: Issues for cross-national survey research. *International Journal of Social Research Methodology*, 2(2), 125–140. https://doi. org/10.1080/136455799295096

Harris, S., & Dowling, M. (*forthcoming*). *Sport Participation and Olympic Legacies: A Comparative Study*. Routledge.

Henry, I., Amara, M., Al-Tauqi, M., & Lee, P. C. (2005). A typology of approaches to comparative analysis of sports policy. *Journal of Sport Management*, 19, 480–496.

Henry, I., Dowling, M., Ko, L. M., & Brown, P. (2020). Challenging the new orthodoxy: a critique of SPLISS and variable-oriented approaches to comparing sporting nations. In *European Sport Management Quarterly*. https://doi.org/10.1080/16184742.202 0.1719428

Hofstede, G. (1998). A case for comparing apples with oranges: International differences in values. *International Journal of Comparative Sociology*, 39(1). 16-31.

Houlihan, B. (1997). *Sport, Policy and Politics: A Comparative Analysis*. Routledge.

Houlihan, B., & Green, M. (2008). *Comparative Elite Sport Policy: Systems, Structures, and Public Policy*. Routledge.

Houlihan, B., Tan, T., & Green, M. (2010). Policy transfer and learning from the west: Elite basketball development in the People's Republic of China. *Journal of Sport and Social Issues*, 34, 4-28. https://doi.org/10.1177/0193723509358971

Hug, S. (2003). Selection Bias in Comparative Research: The Case of Incomplete Data Sets. Political Analysis, 11(3), 255–274. https://doi.org/10.1093/pan/mpg014

Jackman, R. W. (1985). Cross-National Statistical Research and the Study of Comparative Politics. *American Journal of Political Science*, 29, 161-182. https://doi.org/10.2307/2111217

Johnson, T. P. (1998). Approaches to Equivalence in Cross-Cultural and Cross-National Survey Research. *ZUMA-Nachrichten Spezial*, 3, 1–40.

Jowell, R. (1998). How Comparative is Comparative Research? *American Behavioral Scientist*, 42(2), 168–177. https://doi.org/10.1177/0002764298042002004

Kihl, L., Slack, T., & Hinings, B. (1992). Institutionally specific design archetypes: a framework for understanding change in national sport organizations. *International Review for the Sociology of Sport*, 27(4), 343–368. https://doi.org/10.1177/101269029202700405

Kohn, M. L. (1987). Cross-national research as an analytical strategy. *American Sociological Review*, 52, 713–731. https://www.jstor.org/stable/2095831

Kohn, M. L. (1989). *Cross-National Research in Sociology*. SAGE Publications.

Kuhn, T. (1970). *Structure of scientific revolutions* (2nd ed.). Chicago University Press.

Landman, T., & Carvalho, E. (2017). *Issues and Methods in Comparative Politics* (4th ed.). Routledge.

Laswell, H. (1868). The future of the comparative method. *Comparative Politics*, 1(1), 3–18. https://www.jstor.org/stable/421372

Leavy, P. (2017). *Research Design: Quantitative, Qualitative and Mixed Methods, and Community-Based Participatory Approaches*. The Guildford Press.

Lijphart, A. (1971). Comparative politics and the comparative method. *American Political Science Review*, 65(3), 682–93. https://doi.org/10.2307/1955513

Lincoln, Y., & Guba, E. (1985). *Naturalistic Inquiry*. SAGE Publications.

Mayan, M. (2009). *Essentials of Qualitative Inquiry*. Left Coast Press.

Mills, M., van de Bunt, G., & de Bruijn, J. (2006). Comparative Research: Persistent Problems and Promising Solutions. *International Sociology*, 21(5), 619–631. https://doi.org/10.1177/0268580906067833

Mullen, M. (1995). Diagonising measurement equivalence in cross-national research. *Journal of International Business Studies,* 26(3), 573-596. https://doi.org/10.1057/palgrave.jibs.8490187

Oakley, B., & Green, M. (2001). Still playing the game at arm's length? The selective re-investment in British sport, 1995-2000. *Managing Leisure*, 6(2), 74–94. https://doi.org/10.1080/713777657

Øyen, E. (1990). *Comparative Methodology: Theory and Practice in International Social Research*. SAGE Publications.

Øyen, E. (2004). *Living with imperfect comparisons*. P. Kennett (ed). *A Handbook of Comparative Social Policy* (pp. 276-291). Edward Elgar.

Patton, M. (2002). *Qualitative Research and Evaluation Methods*. SAGE Publications.

Petry, K., Steinbach, D., & Tokarski, W. (2004). Sport systems in the countries of the European Union: similarities and differences. *European Journal for Sport and Society*, 1, 15–21. https://doi.org/10.1080/16138171.2004.11687744

Phillips, C., & Burbules, N. (2000). *Philosophical, Theory and Educational Research*. Rowman & Littlefield.

Popper, K. (1963). *Conjectures and Refutations* (1st ed.). Routledge.

Przeworski, A., & Teune, H. (1966). Equivalence in Cross-National Research. *The Public Opinion Quarterly*, 30(4), 551–568.

Przeworski, A., & Teune, H. (1970). *The Logic of Comparative Social Inquiry*. Wiley-Interscience.

Ragin, C. (1987). *The Comparative Method: Moving Beyond Qualitative and Quantitative Strategies*. University of California Press.

Ragin, C. (2006). How to Lure Analytic Social Science Out of the Doldrums: Some Lessons from Comparative Research. *International Sociology*, 21(5), 633–646. https://doi.org/10.1177/0268580906067834

Ragin, C. (2014). *The Comparative Method: Moving Beyond Qualitative and Quantitative Strategies* (2nd ed.). University of California Press.

Ragin, C., & Zaret, D. (1983). Theory and Method in Comparative Research: Two Strategies. *Social Forces*, 61(3), 731–754.

Rihoux, B. (2006). Qualitative Comparative Analysis (QCA) and Related Systematic Comparative Methods: Recent Advances and Remaining Challenges for Social Science Research. *International Sociology*, 21(5), 679–706. https://doi.org/10.1177/0268580906067836

Rihoux, B., & Ragin, C. (2012). Configurational Comparative Methods: Qualitative Comparative Analysis (QCA) and Related Techniques. SAGE. https://doi.org/10.4135/9781452226569

Riordan, J. (1978). *Sport Under Communism*. Hurst.

Riordan, J, & Jones, R. (1999). *Sport and Physical Education in China*. E&FN SPON.

Sabatier, P., & Jenkins-Smith. (1993). *Policy Change and Learning: An Advocacy Coalition Approach*. Westview Press.

Sartori, G. (1970). Concept Misinformation in Comparative Politics. *American Political Science Review*, 64(4), 1033–1053. https://doi.org/10.2307/1958356

Sartori, G. (1994). Compare Why and How: Comparing, Miscomparing and the Comparative Method. In M. Dogan & A. Kazancigil. (eds). *Comparing Nations: Concepts, Strategies, Substance* (pp. 14–34). Blackwell.

Schuster, J. M. (2007). Participation Studies and Cross-National Comparison: Proliferation, Prudence, and Possibility. *Cultural Trends*, 16(2), 99–196. https://doi.org/10.1080/09548960701299815

Senge, P. (1990). *The Fifth Discipline: The Art and Practice of the Learning Organization*. Doubleday.

Slack, T., & Hinings, B. (1994). Institutional Pressures and Isomorphic Change: An Empirical Test. *Organization Studies*, 15(6), 803–827. https://doi.org/10.1177/017084069401500602

Smelser, N. (1976). *Comparative Methods in the Social Sciences*. Prentice-Hall.

Smith, B. (2018). Generalizability in qualitative research: misunderstandings, opportunities and recommendations for the sport and exercise sciences. *Qualitative Research in Sport, Exercise and Health*, 10(1), 137–149. https://doi.org/10.1080/2159676X.2017.1393221

Stegmueller, D. (2011). Apples and Oranges? The problem of equivalence in comparative research. *Political Analysis*, 19(4), 471–487. https://doi.org/10.1093/pan/mpr028

Teune, H. (1990). Comparing countries: lessons learned. In E. Øyen (ed.). *Comparative Methodology: Theory and Practical in International Social Research* (pp. 38–62). SAGE Publications.

Truyens, J., De Bosscher, V., Heyndels, B., & Westerbeek, H. (2014). A resource-based perspective on countries' competitive advantage in elite athletics. *International*

Journal of Sport Policy and Politics, 6(3), 459–489. https://doi.org/10.1080/19406
940.2013.839954

Truyens, J., De Bosscher, V., & Sotiriadou, P. (2016). An analysis of countries' organizational resources, capacities, and resource configurations in athletics. *Journal of Sport Management*, 30(5), 566-585. https://doi.org/10.1123/jsm.2015-0368

Van Deth, J. W. (2006). Equivalence in comparative political research. In: J. Van Deth (ed.). *Comparative Politics: The Problem of Equivalence* (pp. 1–19). Routledge.

Verba S, Nie N., & Kim J. (1978). *Participation and Political Equality: A Seven Nation Comparison.* Cambridge University Press

Wagner, U., & Hanstad, D. V. (2011). Scandinavian perspectives on doping – a comparative policy analysis in relation to the international process of institutionalizing anti-doping. *International Journal of Sport Policy*, 3(3), 355–372. https://doi.org/10.1080/1940
6940.2011.596156

Yin, R. (2017). *Case Study Research and Applications: Design and Methods* (6th ed.). SAGE Publications.

ABOUT THE AUTHORS

Dr Mathew Dowling is a senior lecturer at the Cambridge Centre for Sport and Exercise Sciences at Anglia Ruskin University, UK. He completed his PhD at the University of Alberta, Canada, and is alma mater of Loughborough University, UK. His current research interests focus on the application of organisational and political theory to understand sport organisations and systems. He is widely published in sport policy and politics, organisational change, systemic governance, professionalistion and comparative methods in sport.

Dr Spencer Harris is an associate professor of Sport Management at the University of Colorado, US. He has more than 30 years of experience within the sport development industry and has worked for the University of Hertfordshire, Sport England, and Right to Play. He completed his PhD at Loughborough University, UK. His research interests centre on sport governance and, specifically, the sport–politics–power relationship.

CREDITS

Cover and interior design: Anja Elsen

Layout: ZeroSoft

Cover & part opener image: © AdobeStock

Interior figures: © Mathew Dowling and Spencer Harris

Managing editor: Elizabeth Evans

Copyediting: Stephanie Kramer